PAISLE
AT THE
PICTURES
1950

by
BRIAN
HANNAN

ALSO BY BRIAN HANNAN

The Gunslingers of '69: The Western Movies'
Greatest Year

When Women Ruled Hollywood

The Making of *The Magnificent Seven* – Behind
the Scenes of the Pivotal Western

The Making of *Lawrence of Arabia*

The Making of *The Guns of Navarone*- Revised
Edition (2019) with over 30 Illustrations

Darkness Visible: Hitchcock's Greatest Film

Hitchcock at the Box Office Vol 1: *The 39 Steps*
and *The Lady Vanishes*

Hitchcock at the Box Office Vol 2: *Jamaica Inn*
and *Rebecca*

Hitchcock at the Box Office Vol 3: *Foreign
Correspondent* and *Mr and Mrs Smith*

Coming Back to a Theater Near You: A History of
Hollywood Reissues 1914-2014

In Theaters Everywhere: A History of the
Hollywood Wide Release 1913-2017

First published by Baroliant Press in June 2019.
Reprinted July 2019
Reprinted August 2019
Reprinted September 2019 (twice)
Reprinted November 2019

Baroliant Press, 8 Southfield Ave,
Paisley PA2 8BY

ISBN: 9781909773080

Printed by
Merchant City Print, 261 High St,
Glasgow G4 0QR

CONTACT
Brian Hannan – bhkhannan@aol.com

CONTENTS

Preface

Several years ago, long before I started to write books about the movies, I came into possession of a series of British cinema "Pressbooks" dating from the early 1950s. These were, in effect, marketing tools devised by Hollywood and British studios to help cinema managers sell individual movies to the general public. These publications varied in size from a basic A4 four-page black-and-white effort (example, *The Last Page* starring George Brent and Diana Dors) to glossy landscape-sized brochures running to 24- or 28-pages (example, Walt Disney's *Treasure Island* starring Robert Newton or *Return to Paradise* starring Gary Cooper).

These Pressbooks fulfilled three purposes. The first was to fill the said manager with enthusiasm for the picture and encourage him/her to book it. Secondly, it provided those charged with the local marketing of a film long after any media hullabaloo surrounding a premiere had died away with the necessary artwork to place their own advertisements in local newspapers such as the *Paisley Daily Express*. Thirdly, and most crucially, they presented a huge range of promotional ideas that a manager could adopt to promote the film. These might range from tie-ins with an umbrella retailer (*Singin' in the Rain*) or local clothes store (any film where Robert Mitchum wore a suit) or a competition to find the best kids Wild West outfit

Based on a novel by James Hadley Chase, *The Last Page* was known in the United States as *Man Bait*.

(*Lost Stage Valley*) with the notion that all such ideas would be quickly gobbled up by local newspapers and provide "free" advertising for the forthcoming picture. I had seen so many of these – I had over 700 Pressbooks –

with all sorts of ideas running from the clever to the zany to the downright preposterous that I had got to wondering if cinema managers in this country ever took advantage of these marketing gimmicks and, if so, how and how often.

So I went down to the Paisley Central Library and began looking up copies of the *Paisley Daily Express* from 1950 to 1954. What I had not realised was that a) the newspaper industry at that time was still reeling from the after-effects of paper rationing in the Second World War and that b) any spare photographic coverage would be given over to supporting loyal local readers by covering their weddings rather than being duped into providing commercial organisations with free advertising. The upshot was that, after trawling through 1,500 daily issues of the *Paisley Daily Express* (it published six days a week) for these years I had not found a single example of what I was looking for.

However, out of curiosity, I had kept track of all the films showing in the town's cinemas, which were advertised every day in a classified section on the front page. And when I came to examine my extensive notes I realised I was sitting on a treasure trove of data. As far as I am aware no one has been foolhardy enough to undertake a five-year data collection investigation such as this. So I thought that a book on the cinemagoing habits of one town might make an interesting project. It would provide a fascinating insight into moviegoing habits and revive memories of a glorious period when cinemas were invariably full rather than half-empty and when going to

9

the cinema was a weekly treat for virtually everyone. But rather than covering half a decade, I started at the beginning and examined what Paisley was watching in 1950.

Introduction

In 1950 Paisley had eight cinemas and between them in that year they showed a total of 1,255 films (including repeat showings and cinemas sharing product). Some films ran for a whole week, others three days and, in one particular cinema, just for two. Filmgoers were treated to musicals, westerns, dramas, comedies, film noir and a variety of smaller genres. Pictures featuring big stars like Spencer Tracy and John Wayne were as likely to be seen as smaller pictures headlined by comedy duo Abbott and Costello or a series like the "Ma and Pa Kettle" films. Films were shown on their own and in double bills. The quality of the cinema varied from the top-ranked Kelburne and Regal to the more inexpensive West End and Palladium. Throughout Britain, cinema-going remained at a peak with 1.349 billion admissions in 1950. However, film-making in the United States was in a trough, the dismantling of the Hollywood studio system wreaking havoc on production, while, conversely, Hollywood had embarked on heavy investment in British films, mostly as a method of activating the millions of dollars frozen in British bank accounts by the U.K. government during and after the Second World War, but partly because it was cheaper. In turn, to protect the home-grown industry, the government maintained a production quota system, although, in truth, that resulted in too many British films with low production values ("quota quickies"). The most pernicious destructive force – television – was still in its

11

infancy. So, this was a boom time for cinemagoers with a huge number of films on show, Paisley averaging 23 per every week.

Unlike now when the release of films involves a more democratic process with every major film launched in every multiplex in Britain at exactly the same time, a completely different system was in operation in 1950. Movie release followed a hierarchical system whereby films were launched in London's prestigious West End cinemas and then over a period of time wound their way around the country. Circulation was limited by the number of copies (prints) of films available. Making prints was an expensive business and one print was expected to service dozens of cinemas until it was completely worn out. There were far fewer prints of each film than now so smaller locations like Paisley had to wait their turn to see the new films. Like every other town, Paisley had some cinemas which only showed new films and major reissues of older ones and others which concentrated on showing repeats of both new films and older ones. A film would open in a "first run" cinema for three or six days and then several weeks or months later would reappear in one of the "second-run" houses for a period of two or three days. Films did not, like today, run for weeks on end until demand diminished. They were scheduled to run in a cinema for a specified period and once that time was up they were yanked off the screen even if they were doing terrific business. So audiences had to be quick off the

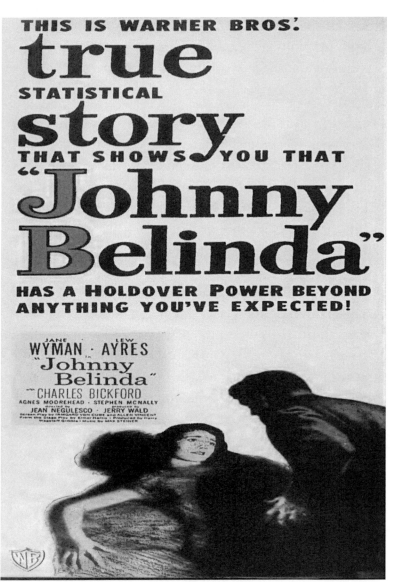

Nominated for 12 Oscars, Jane Wyman as Best Actress was the only winner for *Johnny Belinda*.

mark. If they missed a new movie first time round they would certainly get another bite at the cherry, but after a second-run appearance a film would be gone and usually forever.

Paisley in 1950 was Scotland's largest town with 93,000 inhabitants (according to the 1951 census) and situated several miles to the west of Scotland's biggest metropolis Glasgow. Industry centred around weaving and textiles. The Coats mills were famous throughout the world for their "Paisley Pattern" materials but there were also factories producing chocolate, tobacco, jam, and cornflour as well as heavy industry such as shipbuilding. The town boasted an abbey and a cathedral and other historical landmarks like the Coats Memorial Church with an observatory. The city centre was set on a river, and there was a bustling retail environment and, in the absence of the ubiquitous supermarkets that dominate today's high streets, shops of every description.

You could buy fish and meat from McKerachers, get your carpets cleaned at Bell's and drop your dry cleaning off at The Valet Service in the High St. For sweets you could head for the Confectionary Quality Shop. Clothes were available from Wilkinsons ("trousers and jackets") in Broomlands St, Cochran's in Gauze St, and Blair's and Smith's Ladies and Gent's Tailors in Wellmeadow St. Clothes retailers located in the High St included Hipps, Dalziel's, Stanley Bros and Jean's Fashion Shop. Other shops sold more specialist items: waterproofs could be purchased from The Rubber Shop in Orr St, bedding from

John Walker in the High St and John Park in Canal St, and shoes from Manfield in the High St or Dykes in Gauze St. Pianos were available from Benzie & Co and Wm. Thompson in Causeyside St although the former also offered radios and suites of furniture. There was Clark's Tea Rooms in Glasgow Road and Bailey's Wine Merchants in Gilmour St. Gilloughley, selling watches and jewellery, had two branches, one in Gauze St and a second in Causeyside St. Clydesdale in the High St was at the technological forefront, with television sets for sale. Bruce's had a furniture shop in the High St, Grant's one at The Cross, also the location for Anderson's Fire Places. You could buy prams from Glasgow's in Cotton St and have your eyes tested at Horsburgh in the High St. Paisley Motors in Causeyside advertised automobiles and Oddfellow's Hall was often used for general "sales."

Going to the cinema was far more popular then than now. There were nearly 12 times as many cinema admissions in 1950 as there are these days (cinema admissions in 2017 totaled just 117 million). What people went to see and what they were prevented from seeing is the subject of this book.

Chapter One: Paisley's Cinemas

In 1950 Paisley had eight cinemas. This was a surprisingly high proportion per head of population and, unlike other towns and cities, all but one of the cinemas were located in the city centre.

The Kelburne, La Scala, and Regal were the most important. They specialised in first-run films and so were the most expensive. The Kelburne was situated at 53 Glasgow Road. It had been opened in 1933 by A.B. King and contained 1,784 seats. The marble-fronted La Scala Picture House, at Paisley Cross, had opened on September 19, 1921. It was refurbished in 1929 to allow for the introduction of sound equipment, the first talkie being *Show Boat*. The name was shortened to just La Scala in 1945 and it also boasted a very popular tea room. The Regal at 95 High St, at the corner of Lady Lane, was built by the Associated British Cinema (ABC) circuit and launched with *The House of Rothschild* starring George Arliss on November 26, 1934. One of its main attractions was an organ with an illuminated console.

The other five cinemas were the Picture House, Palladium, West End, New Alex and Astoria. The Picture House at 23 High St, designed by architect George A. Boswell, was the oldest of the town's cinemas still in operation, having first opened its doors in 1912. In February 1930, it was rebuilt in the more modern Art

Deco style, increasing seating capacity to 2,281. The cinema boasted a fountain at the entrance. The remains of the B-listed façade can still be seen at the entrance to the Paisley Centre shopping mall. The Astoria was located in Lawn St, The Palladium in Weighhouse Close just behind the High St and the West End in Broomlands St.

The Alexandra Cinema in Orr St was the only cinema that operated outside the city centre, although it was barely half a mile away, opposite the original Royal Alexandra Hospital (hence the cinema's name). It opened in December 1923 and when refurbished in 1938-1939 was renamed the New Alex. Apart from the New Alex, the cinemas formed a relatively compact unit, barely a mile-and-a-half separating the Kelburne at one end of the town from the West End at the other.

Apart from the Regal, run by ABC, and the Kelburne, run by Caledonian Associated Cinemas, all the theaters were independent. Significantly, there was neither an Odeon nor a Gaumont, the other two major UK-wide chains.

The cinemas competed for the leisure customer with the Paisley Theatre which put on plays, musicals and variety shows and the Ice Rink which hosted ballroom dancing and boxing matches such as Peter Keenan vs. Bunty Doran or wrestling evenings with attractions such as The Ghoul vs. Sandy Orford on the bill.

Single Films vs. Double Bills

The 1,255 films screened in 1950 were divided into programmes of single- and double-bills. Every programme, whether comprising one or two films, also contained a newsreel and trailers and sometimes a cartoon or serial. In general, the number of programmes remained relatively constant, averaging 60 per month, and never falling below 56 (June and December) while reaching a maximum of 67 in June. In only three months of the year (May, June and December) did the total number of films shown dip below 100, and the average monthly output was 104. Screenings peaked in March and July with 114 films shown in each month.

As cinemagoers demanded value for money, the bulk of these programmes were double bills. While main features might run upwards of 90 minutes with many approaching or exceeding the two-hour mark, the supporting features were rarely as long, many (known as "B" features) being made to a specific length in order to act as the supporting film in an overall programme. However, due to the general product shortage, many movies that were intended to fulfill the B-films criteria in the United States turned up as the main feature in Britain. The biggest advantage of a programme consisting of one film rather than two was that a cinema could have four or five showings in the one day rather than two or three.

The number of double-bills far outweighed single bills. Nearly three times as many double-bills were programmed

18

than single bills, 73.4 per cent compared to 26.6 per cent. The number of single bills was at its highest in November (22), July (20) and October (19) and at its lowest in September (9), January (12) and April (12). A total of 50 double bills was shown in each of March and September.

Films were shown on a "continuous programme" basis which meant that the movies ran non-stop without an intermission or break between the movies. Some people saw the supporting feature first before the main picture was projected, but others watched the movies the other way round. Equally, there was nothing stopping a customer coming in halfway through a movie and then staying on through the complete programme to catch the other half of the first film. The length of programmes varied. For example, taking one day at random, the complete show at the La Scala lasted three-and-three-quarter-hours; for the Regal it was three-and-a-quarter-hours; and for the Kelburne it was under three hours, just two hours and 50 minutes.

Out of the eight cinemas, only half – Regal, Kelburne, La Scala and Palladium – even considered running single bills. But this was not an exclusive policy and, for example, single bills, in fact, accounted for less than 38 per cent of the programmes for this cinematic quartet in January 1950. That month, for example, the Kelburne ran 14 days of single bills, the Regal 12 days, the Palladium 10 days and La Scala eight days. The Kelburne programmed in biopic *The Dolly Sisters* starring Betty Grable for two days (the cinema being closed for the first day of the run for the New Year's Day holiday), then six straight days each of Anna Neagle and husband Michael Wilding in British musical *Maytime in Mayfair* followed by Hollywood swashbuckler *The Three Musketeers* starring Lana Turner and Gene Kelly. The Regal single-bill attractions were also *Maytime in Mayfair* and *The Three Musketeers*. The Palladium ran five single-bills, each lasting for two days: Bob Hope comedy *Sorrowful Jones*, Alan Ladd as *The Great Gatsby*, Ray Milland in film noir *The Contact Man*, William Holden in western *The Streets of Laredo* and Tyrone Power in Henry King's historical adventure *Captain from Castile*. The La Scala showed romantic comedy *Two Girls and a Sailor* starring Van Johnson and June Allyson for two days (the annual holiday truncating the run), Howard Hawks musical-comedy *A Song Is Born* starring Danny Kaye and Virginia Mayo for three days and comedy western *The Kissing Bandit* starring Frank Sinatra and Kathryn Grayson for another three.

And you would be wrong to assume that the film shown on its own was closer in length to a double bill or that somehow the audience was not going to be short-changed in terms of movie length. Only *Captain from Castile*, clocking in at 140 minutes, could be considered a long picture. Only two others crossed the two-hour mark, *The Three Musketeers* by five minutes, *Two Girls and a Sailor* by four. *Sorrowful Jones* did not even last 90 minutes, coming in two minutes shorter, while the running time for *The Great Gatsby* was 91 minutes, *The Streets of Laredo*

Top: Jean Peters co-starred with Tyrone Power in *Captain from Castile*. Bottom: Bob Hope and Lucille Ball in *Sorrowful Jones*.

and *The Contact Man* both 93 minutes and *Maytime in Mayfair* 94 minutes. Of course, then, as now, length was not everything. An audience would be happy to sit through a film it considered highly entertaining regardless of running time. Equally, a cinema manager would have to be sure of his ground to deny the cinemagoer a double bill.

By comparison, it is worth considering the total length of the double bills running in these cinemas, again using January as the example. In fact, there were as many differences in terms of running time in double bills as there had been with single bills. The double bill at the Kelburne of Johnny Weissmuller jungle adventure *Jungle Jim* coupled with *Blondie's Big Deal* only totaled 137 minutes – less than the running time of *Captain from Castile*. At the La Scala Alan Ladd film noir *Chicago Deadline* and British comedy *The Melody Club* lasted 149 minutes while western *The Younger Brothers* and *Princess O'Rourke* lasted 172 minutes, exactly the same time as the Regal's combination of British war picture *Landfall* and drama *Bad Boy* while the latter cinema's double bill of Doris Day musical *My Dream Is Yours* teamed with *The House Across the Street* was 170 minutes. However, it is worth noting that only one of these pictures – *My Dream Is Yours* – ran for longer than any of the films chosen for single bill presentation.

Since the price of admission to a film or films showing at any particular cinema did not vary, it is worth considering whether audiences felt better value for money was to be had from seeing one prestigious production rather than two more lightweight attractions and whether the length of a programme played any part in their decision to opt for a cinema showing a single bill as opposed to a double bill. As you can judge from the examples given above, the films chosen to be shown on their own generally were bigger-budgeted films with stars of the calibre of Anna Neagle, Bob Hope, Lana Turner and Tyrone Power although, as instanced by Alan Ladd, perceived marquee attraction did not determine whether a film was shown in a single- or double-bill.

First Run vs. Second Run

Six of the Paisley cinemas primarily showed first run films. These were the Kelburne, Regal, La Scala, Picture House, New Alex and West End. A pecking order clearly existed with the Regal, Kelburne and La Scale getting the pick of the first-run movies, although this might be at the expense of being forced to show a film for six days rather than three. The three big cinemas alternated between films shown over six days and three days and between single bills and double bills. The other cinemas showed films exclusively in double bills. In January 1950, for example, the Kelburne offered a total of eight programmes, two single bills for six days each, four double bills for three days, one single bill for two days and, unusually, one for one day, and even more unusually that was a Sunday, this being a charity performance of the old John Wayne

Above: Sessue Hayakawa, a huge star in the U.S. during the silent era, co-starred in *Tokyo Joe*.

James Stewart had not made a western in more than a decade when he took the leading role in *Winchester '73*.

picture *Without Reservations* (1946). The Regal limited itself to five programmes, three single bills running for six days, one single bill for five days (one day lost to the holiday) and a double bill for three days. The La Scala had eight programmes, one double bill lasting six days, two single bills running three days, and five double bills with three-day tenures. At the other end of the scale, the New Alex, West End and Picture House each showed nine programmes, all double bills that ran for three days.

The two second run houses were the Astoria and the Palladium. A visitor to the former in January was offered a diet of double bills each available for three days, a total of nine programmes in the first month of the year. However, films were only seen at the Palladium for two days at a time, so this meant in January that 13 programmes were advertised, eight as double bills and five as single bills.

Opening Times

In 1950 movies were shown every day of the week except Sunday apart from an occasional Charity Show screening of an old film. The bigger cinemas held their first screenings in the afternoon between 1pm and 3pm, depending on the programme. (Not all cinemas advertised screening times in the daily newspaper). Some theatres managed to show three full double bills a day, others ran three showings of the main feature and two of the support.

Others only showed one programme and for a big film this could be four times a day. Some cinemas closed "for refurbishment" for a week or ten days in the summer, coinciding with the local holiday. All Paisley theatres remained open on Xmas Day. The Kelburne hosted a midnight showing in the run-up to New Year's Eve.

The first screening in the largest cinemas was generally between 1pm and 2pm. Double bills could last as long as three-and-three-quarter hours, or as little as under three hours. Programme timings were altered every week according to what was playing. In one typical week, the La Scala showed the main feature at 1.45pm, 5.30pm and 9.15pm with the supporting feature running in between at 3.10pm and 6.55pm. The same system applied to the Regal: main feature at 2.40pm, 5.55pm and 9.10pm, support showing twice. The Kelburne employed an alternative approach, scheduling complete double bill programmes, the support at 2.05pm, 4.55pm and 7.50pm ahead of the main feature at 3.25pm, 6.15pm and 9.05pm. The Picture House, following the same system as the Kelburne, however had downright curious timings: the support at 2.51pm, 5.24pm and 7.57pm with the main attraction on screen at 3.50pm, 6.23pm and 8.56pm. Perhaps this was a device to ensure customers turned up on time. Compared to the current fashion, start times of the feature related to the actual projection time of the film rather than the advertisements and trailers. In some cinemas, the times of the trailers and the newsreel were shown on a display board.

Programming

In 1950 the bulk of the cinemas changed programmes midweek. Movies, typically, ran Mon-Wed and then Thu-Sat. However, the Regal would generally play a film Mon-Sat while the Kelburne and La Scala oscillated between one-week showings and split-week programming. The Palladium changed its programme three times a week, on Mondays, Wednesdays and Fridays. The maximum run for a film was one week. As previously stated, there was no leeway in this regard. Once a run was complete, the film was removed from the cinema, the print headed for another picture house. So, unlike today or later in the 1950s and 1960s, no films were retained beyond these three-day or six-day maximums, nor did any return to the same cinema for another showing.

Full-week single bills were presented with a "full supporting programme" which generally comprised a short travelogue and/or cartoon and a newsreel. Single bills maximised box office potential as cinemas could programme in four showings a day and not have to share the receipts with another film. Serials (see below) were shown in some cinemas and, in fact, attracted considerable attention, the West End and the New Alex advertised (at a time when such advertisements were exceedingly rare) the forthcoming *Flash Gordon* on the front page of the *Paisley Daily Express*, and restricted the showings to the Thu-Sat performances, one episode a week. One cinema always advertised that it had organ music. The ABC Minors probably ran continuously but were not always

28

THERE ARE *20* GUNS BETTING THEY'LL NEVER CROSS THE BORDER TONIGHT*!*

UNIVERSAL-INTERNATIONAL presents *Fred* MacMURRAY *Claire* TREVOR

Her first role since winning the Academy Award for "Key Largo"

Borderline

Above: Claire Trevor had won Best Supporting Actress in her previous film *Key Largo* (1948) while Fred MacMurray had starred in classic film noir *Double Indemnity* (1944).

advertised within the classified ads. Newsreels were also promoted underneath a cinema's main classified advertisement when they contained a football match such as the Scottish Cup Final or a boxing match such as

Woodcock vs. Savold or the christening of Princess Anne. Occasionally, a live event would be incorporated into the evening programme – the Kelburne had a "Revuette" called "the Kelburne Papers", the New Alex had the "Paisley Bonnie Lassies" (from the Anchor and Ferguslie Mills), and the Regal, as part of a nationwide tie-up, held a local heat for the *Neptune's Daughter* Beauty Contest in midsummer and also hosted the local heats for the Donald Peers Singing Contest.

Product Sharing

Cinemas shared films on a regular basis. Sometimes this was a "big" film that would run for a week at each location. Other times it would be a double bill showing for three days. In fact, product sharing was so rife that there were only 33 days in the entire year when two or more cinemas were not sharing product. Apart from the Astoria and the Palladium, all cinemas were involved in this practice. For some it was a consistent way of running their business, for others it was less common. The two houses which most frequently engaged in product sharing were the New Alex and the West End, which were under the same management. The New Alex exclusively shared product with the West End, but the latter cinema also enjoyed simultaneous screenings with the Picture House. The Kelburne shared product mostly with the Regal for six-day runs but also occasionally, usually for three days, with the La Scala, the Picture House and the West End.

The New Alex and the West End ran a total of 37 programmes, predominantly double bills, at the same time, sometimes, such as in August, as many as six times a month, other months, such as October, as few as one. Only one picture, *To the Victor*, was shown in both cinemas without a support. Also once, when the New Alex screened *Dark Secret* on its own, the West End added the *Ghost and the Guest* as a support. The West End shared 27 programmes with the Picture House, June and December the busiest months, with five and four programmes, respectively. Again, in the main, these were double bills.

But there were some anomalies. When *Yes Sir, That's My Baby/Undertow* was shown, the former was advertised as the main feature at the West End with the latter given pride of place at the Picture House. The same process was repeated for *Brute/The Devil's Hand* and for *Magic Town/Race Street*. One programme enjoyed a six-day run, *Champion/Fabulous Joe*, while *D.O.A.* was screened in both cinemas without a support. Equally, on rare occasions, the managers opted for a different support. *Landfall* was seen with *Valiant Hombre* at the West End but *The Duke of Chicago* at the Picture House.

Twice the Picture House was comfortable running the main feature without a support, and for *Ellen* the West End added *Man of Courage*, while *Johnny Holliday* was supplemented by *Jailbirds*.

Battleground was nominated for six Oscars including Best Picture.

When the Kelburne combined with the Regal it was always for pictures running for six days. These were mostly shown without a support. The two cinemas linked up 14 times in 1950 for prestigious offerings such as swashbuckler *The Three Musketeers*, thriller *The Third Man*, war picture *Battleground* and musical *On the Town*. Once, a double bill was shown in both houses, *The Pride of Kentucky/The Girl from Jones Beach*, and when *Under Capricorn* was chosen by both, the Regal decided to add *P.C. 49* as a support. The 15 teamings of the Kelburne and the La Scala, on the other hand, were only for three-day runs, a mixture of double bills and solo features that

32

included western *Broken Arrow* starring James Stewart, Ingrid Bergman as *Joan of Arc*, comedies *The Great Lover/Big Brown Eyes,* Barbara Stanwyck in *No Man of Her Own*, film noir *Night and the City* and *Panic in the Streets*. The only notable anomaly was that Disney's reinterpretation of *Treasure Island* was shown for three days at Xmas at the Kelburne and six days at the La Scala. Simultaneous openings at the Kelburne and the Picture House were less frequent, only six times during the year. *Jolson Sings Again* ran for six days at both houses while *Good Sam/Strange Bargain* ran six days at the Picture House but only three at the Kelburne. All others were for three days. The Kelburne showed *All the King's Men* without a support, but the Picture House added *Three Ham on Rye*, and when *Mark of the Gorilla* also went solo the Picture House appended *Sea Wall*. When the Kelburne went into the sharing business with the West End, four times in 1950, always in three-day runs, they differed over the need for a support. Supporting *The Chiltern Hundreds*, the Kelburne offered *They Meet Again* while for the West End it was *Borrowed Trouble*; and with *Train of Events*, the former showed *Dinner at the Ritz* and the latter *White Stallion*. For *Come to the Stables*, the Kelburne dispensed with a support while the other cinema reprised *Rope of Sand*. Admittedly, these choices may have been forced upon the theatres, if there were not sufficient prints of the support to go round.

Mark of the Gorilla was the fourth in the "Jungle Jim" series.

How the Public Found Out What Was On

Every cinema had poster displays announcing what was running that week and possibly also for the following week and the public, out visiting the shops or catching a bus or a train, would view these advertisements in the course of their daily lives. No doubt eager film fans would make a weekly pilgrimage to the fronts of all cinemas to find out details of what was on.

But the easiest way to view the week's fare was to scan the front page of the *Paisley Daily Express.* This was a broadsheet with three editions a day ("at 2, 3, and 5 o'clock"). The paper had seven columns per page. In 1950 the editions between Monday and Thursday comprised four pages, while on Friday and Saturday this generally rose to six pages. There was still a newsprint shortage, and paper was rationed, but how big a part this played in the size of the *Paisley Daily Express* is unknown.

Unlike now, the front page was not devoted to news, but was covered entirely by small ads, a mixture of lineage (adverts that ran for two or three lines without a headline), box advertisements for shops and goods, and classified advertisements such as Situations Vacant and Public Announcements and, in the summer, advertisements for hotels and boarding houses ranging from Aberdeen in the north to Blackpool and Whitley Bay in England and Bangor and Belfast in Northern Ireland. In terms of editorial, the newspaper was a typically local one, mostly covering events taking place in the area with a smattering of national news, and there would be regular items of Church News, football reports, as well as items announcing "New Books in Library." The few photographs were mainly devoted to coverage of local weddings.

Prominent among the front page classified advertisements were ones for the cinemas. In fact, these stood out on the front page since they ran in a block every single day on the central two columns, one cinema underneath the other, and were both the biggest and boldest adverts on that page. They were all the same size although the typeface varied according to whether a cinema was showing just one film that week or had a split programme and whether these programmes comprised one film or two. The advertisements, small though they were, always specified the stars, usually the male and female leads, of the films. Some cinemas ran the same advertisement all week, others, offering split programmes, amended the advertisements mid-week. On Saturdays the New Alex and the West End would advertise the next week's programme while the other theaters stuck to the current week's fare. The fact that a theater was showing a single bill automatically pushed up the size of typeface, so, in essence, since these invariably ran all week, the biggest film of the week was promoted in the biggest type size and was, therefore, the film title that automatically attracted the most attention on the page.

Curiously, there was also a democratic process in play. Although the block of advertisements occupied the same space every day of the week, the cinemas rotated, so that one day the cinema at the top of the column might be the Regal, the next day the Astoria, the next day the Kelburne and so on.

It was rare to see a display advertisement for a film. Display advertisements, in any case, usually ran inside the paper on the outside sections of the page. Nor were they of the sizes commonly used today. There were no full-page advertisements and no half-page ones either. In 1950 only one cinema, the Regal, ran display advertisements for feature films, but on a very limited scale. These were for: British picture *Maytime in Mayfair* starring Anna Neagle (twice); Robert Donat in *Cure for Love* (once); *It's a Great Feeling* starring Dennis Morgan and newcomer Doris Day (twice), *Young Man of Music* starring Kirk Douglas and Doris Day (twice), controversial drama *Lost Boundaries* (once), and British prisoner-of-war film *The Wooden Horse* (twice). If the Regal ran two adverts, one would be placed in the week before the movie was shown, the other once the run had begun.

The New Alex and the West End were the only other cinemas that advertised, but then only for serials. *Flash Gordon* was advertised in advance of its appearance with, as mentioned above, a front page advertisement. *Dick Tracy* was later given the same treatment as was *The Purple Monster Strikes.* Unusually, compared to feature films, the serials were more heavily advertised, *Dick Tracy* receiving six insertions, *The Purple Monster Strikes* four. Oddly enough, there were also, in very limited style,

37

advertisements for films showing in Glasgow: *The Third Man* at the La Scala and *Bicycle Thieves* at the Cosmo.

Below: *East Side, West Side* was one of six movies starring Barbara Stanwyck made in 1949-1950.

There were also two series of display advertisements appearing on a semi-regular basis that used stars to help promote product and, indirectly, to market forthcoming films. The Max Factor advertisements featured a series of different female stars, the face changing in every successive advertisement, each time incorporating the

38

name of a forthcoming movie. So, for example, Joan Caulfield's face appeared in conjunction with *Dear Wife*, Ava Gardner for *The Great Sinner*, Barbara Stanwyck for *East Side, West Side*, and Susan Hayward for *My Foolish Heart*. Later in the year, the company put more emphasis on the star and instead of using just one photograph, the advertisement ran three. The first recipient of this promotional largesse was Diana Dors.

Local chocolate manufacturer Duncan's also ran a series of advertisements under the generic title of "The Private Lives of the Stars" utilising a succession of British stars, usually in conjunction with a forthcoming movie. These included Rona Anderson, star of *Floodtide* and *Poet's Pub* (twice), "vivacious young star" Joan Greenwood (four times), Valerie Hobson, *Wicked Lady* star Patricia Roc (four times), Jean Kent, Barbara Hale (once) promoting *That Bedside Manner*, Terry Moore (twice) in relation to *He's A Cockeyed Wonder* and Marguerite Chapman (twice) in advance of *Kansas Raiders*.

In addition, other advertisements were aimed at the moviegoer. There was an advertisement for fan magazine *Photoplay* while the national *Daily Express*, in advertising the forthcoming serialisation of the novel *Stromboli*, marketed it around the names of Ingrid Bergman and Roberto Rossellini, so, in some effect, this was a movie tie-in and part of the marketing initiatives that would have been promoted through the Pressbook, although, as previously mentioned, few ideas from studios were used.

The *Paisley Daily Express* also provided free editorial coverage of the films showing locally. Once a week two columns (about one-third of a page) inside the newspaper were given over to a run-down of the week's offerings. Each cinema was granted its own , admittedly relatively small, individual space with a heading while the mini-article supplied the public with relevant information about the movie(s) showing including details of the featured stars and the storyline.

However, that was the extent of editorial coverage in the local newspaper, and it was the same with virtually every other form of entertainment. Although movies never received any other editorial, a play at the local theatre once received coverage of star Jane Hampshire because the play was entitled *Jane Steps Out*.

Otherwise, no use was made in 1950 of the mass of information and showmanship ideas promoted in Pressbooks, except for the one occasion when the Regal became involved in the *Neptune's Daughter* beauty contest, a standard marketing ploy of the period. The only other time a cinema was mentioned on the editorial pages was when there was an attempted break-in at one of the picture houses.

Films in general were only mentioned, again once, in relation to a mobile film unit touring the country showing documentary shorts about industry.

Claudette Colbert was born in France as Claudette Chauchoin. She had been a huge star in the 1930s and more recently *The Egg and I* had featured in the annual Top Ten movies at the box office in 1947. *Bride for Sale* (1949) was a comedy.

41

The Long Wait – Victims of the Distribution Gap

Paisley was not first in line to receive new movies in Scotland. In general, cinemas were in a queue behind Glasgow. With Glasgow only 15 minutes away by train, longer and problems of supply coupled by demand for films from certain stars meant that the reissue vault was raided on a constant basis.

Only 107 films – 8.5 per cent of the total - that were originally released either in the United States or in Britain in 1950 were shown in Paisley in that same year. Even so, there was generally a delay of around six months. Theoretically, at least, there should have been less of a gap between the London premiere and Paisley showing, but that did not always prove the case. As I discovered in my most recent book *In Theaters Everywhere, A History of the Hollywood Wide Release* 1913-2017, the idea of films being released locally in the U.S. at the same time as receiving their first outing in a city like New York – known as "day-and-date" or "day-dating" release - had been part of the distribution pattern in that country for the best part of two decades, but the same idea had not generally caught on in Britain.

However, in 1950, Paisley cinemas twice participated in what was, effectively, a day-and-date release or something akin to it. Jack Warner police drama *The Blue Lamp* opened in June in both London and Paisley and in November the topical American thriller *Deported* starring Marta Toren and Jeff Chandler repeated the trick.

Above: Swedish actress Marta Toren headlined film noir *Deported*
(1950) with the up-and-coming Jeff Chandler.

But most films took longer to travel from London to the sticks. Even films that were shunted around with alacrity still took a mighty long time by today's standards. There was a two-month wait to see British films *Angel with a Trumpet* starring Eileen Herlie and *The Dancing Years,* a musical starring Dennis Price and Giselle Preville, three months for American war blockbuster *Battleground* and British film *Last Holiday* starring Alec Guinness, and four months to see *Appointment with Danger* starring Alan Ladd and British actress Phyllis Calvert.

At the other end of the scale were oldies reissued for the umpteenth time, some just plucked from the catalogue on a one-off basis, others the subject of a concerted reissue following the post-war boom in revivals in the U.S., when several movies made more at the box office on their second go-round. The oldest movie on show dated back to 1931: Laurel and Hardy in *Jailbirds* (aka *Pardon Us*).

Chapter Two: The Top Films in 1950 in Paisley

The ultimate accolade in Paisley was for a film to open on two screens in a six-day run at each. But screen time was so rare that only a dozen films achieved that throughout 1950. Another two films would have achieved it except for the intrusion of the year-end in lopping off one day from each of the theaters. Six movies showed for nine days on initial release, six days in one cinema and three days in the other, the shorter run usually taking place at the start of the week. Two ran for eight days. However, the most common release was one lasting six days, made up either of a six-day run in a single theater or simultaneous three-day runs at two houses. This occurred 131 times during the year. Of the 12-day openers, only two were double bills, while of the six-day openers 81 per cent were double-bills.

In local terms, the top openers were determined as those which ran for the longest period of time on initial release in the town: the films which merited a 12-day showing, six days each in two cinemas. Among the top openers no genre dominated. There were four dramas, two musicals, two adventure pictures, and one each relating to war, comedy, biopic and crime/thriller. However, only a handful of studios risked these big openings. MGM had five films released this way including one from its British division. Warner Brothers also had five, including two British co-productions. The other two came from Columbia and Selznick Releasing Organisation. Given the unequal share of screens accorded British films, in terms of this kind of launch, the domestic product gave a better account of itself. While there were no films whose finance had come solely from this country, Carol Reed's *The Third Man* starring Orson Welles was a demonstrably British product, albeit with American stars. *Maytime in Mayfair* boasted British stars Anna Neagle and Michael Wilding, and was made at the MGM British studios. Alfred Hitchcock's *Under Capricorn* with Ingrid Bergman was made by his own company Transatlantic Pictures with funding from Warner Brothers. A co-production between Associated British Picture Corporation and Warner Brothers, *The Hasty Heart*, had little British about it except for being made at Elstree. It had two American stars, Ronald Reagan and Patricia Neal, although Richard Todd received third-billing.

The other MGM products were big budget items – war film *Battleground*, drama *Little Women* with June Allyson, Margaret O'Brien and Elizabeth Taylor, swashbuckler *The Three Musketeers* headlined by Lana Turner and musical *On the Town* with Gene Kelly and Frank Sinatra. Warner Brothers put out in this fashion Errol Flynn in *The New Adventures of Don Juan* (aka *Adventures of Don Juan* and directed by Vincent Sherman), Danny Kaye comedy *The Inspector General* and the double bill *Pride of Kentucky* (aka *The Story of Seabiscuit*) starring Shirley Temple and *The Girl from Jones Beach* starring Ronald Reagan and Virginia Mayo.

Above: Echoing the famous kiss from *Spellbound* (1945) was promotional material for Alfred Hitchcock's *Under Capricorn* (1949) with Ingrid Bergman and Joseph Cotton who starred in one of the year's Paisley hits *The Third Man* (1949).

Above: *Treasure Island*. Below: *All the King's Men* won three Oscars including Best Picture and Best Actor.

Added to this list should be two films that lost two days out of a potential twelve by coming up against a national holiday and these were Fred Astaire-Ginger Rogers musical *The Berkeleys of Broadway* and Esther Williams and Red Skelton in *Neptune's Daughter*, both Hollywood products.

The half-dozen films that received nine-day showings, six days in one cinema and three days in the other – comprised two single bills and four double bills. The single bills were Robert Rossen drama *All the Kings Men* with Broderick Crawford delivering an Oscar-winning performance and Walt Disney's first British production *Treasure Island*, based on the Robert Louis Stevenson classic and made using funds frozen in British banks, starring Dorset-born Robert Newton and 12-year-old American Bobby Driscoll. Oscar-nominated Kirk Douglas in Mark Robson's hard-hitting boxing drama *Champion* was teamed up with *The Fabulous Joe* about a talking dog starring Walter Abel and Margot Grahame. Glenn Ford and Nina Foch in film noir *The Undercover Man* was supported by *Blondie Hits the Jackpot*, the twenty-seventh film in a series that starred Penny Singleton as the eponymous heroine and Arthur Lake as Dagwood and was based on the popular newspaper comic strip. British comedy *What a Carry On!* with Jimmy Jewel and no relation to the "Carry On" series was accompanied by musical *A Touch of Shamrock* starring Peggy Ryan. Humphrey Bogart and Gloria Grahame headlined Nicholas Ray film noir *In a Lonely Place* with *Father Was a Full Back* starring Fred MacMurray and Maureen O'Hara in tow. Two other programmes would have qualified for this ranking except for losing a day to holidays. These were a single bill of Howard Hawks' *You Can't Sleep Here* (changed for reasons of British delicacy from the better known *I Was a Male War Bride*) starring Cary Grant and Ann Sheridan and the double bill of *The*

Dancing Years and diving adventure *16 Fathoms Deep* starring Lloyd Bridges.

Above: Gregory Peck was nominated for a fourth time for the Best Actor Oscar for war picture *Twelve O'Clock High* (1949) directed by Henry King.

50

.By the standards of the day, since single bills were apt to earn more during their run than double bills courtesy of more screenings and not having to share receipts with another picture, the movies that ran for six days in a single bill programme would be deemed to be next most successful. It is worth contemplating why some of these pictures did not qualify for nine-day or twelve-day exposure. But the simple answer to the question would be precedent. The movies that were shown in two cinemas at once for as long as was possible at the time were generally those which had showed box office power elsewhere and came to Paisley with the promise of further riches. Equally, the fact that they were to be shown without a supporting feature indicated that they still stood out, if only in terms of expectation, from the run of the mill. Even so, the list of some of the titles denied the longer run makes interesting reading.

Assuming no one in the U.K. was interested in baseball, the title of the Frank Sinatra-Esther Williams-Gene Kelly comedy musical *Take Me out to the Ball Game* was changed to *Everybody's Cheering*. Burt Lancaster was an up-and-coming star when he headlined film noir *Rope of Sand* and Judy Garland a major box office attraction when she headlined *In the Good Old Summertime*. Blacklisted Hollywood director Edward Dmytryk's British-made film noir *Obsession* starred Robert Newton and Sally Gray. There were war films: Clark Gable (still the "King of Hollywood") in *Command Decision*, Oscar-nominated Gregory Peck in Henry King's *Twelve O'Clock High* while Terence Young (*Dr No*) directed British effort *They Were Not Divided*. Adventure *Mighty Joe Young*, which won the Oscar for best special effects and starred Terry Moore and Ben Johnson, attempted to cash in on the earlier *King Kong* which had been recently reissued. Three actresses in Elia Kazan's racial drama *Pinky* were nominated for Oscars – star Jeanne Crain and supporting actresses Ethel Barrymore and Ethel Waters. Delmer Daves' post-war drama *To the Victor* put Dennis Morgan on a collision course with collaborator Viveca Lindfors, a Swedish actress making her Hollywood debut. Ingrid Bergman was also Oscar-nominated for her role as *Joan of Arc*. Errol Flynn and Greer Garson came together for the adaptation of the John Galsworthy classic *The Forsyte Saga*. James Cagney put in an incendiary performance in Howard Hawks gangster classic *White Heat* with Virginia Mayo also in sparkling form as his wife. Loretta Young and Celeste Holm played nuns in *Come to the Stable* while Phyllis Calvert popped up as another nun in deadly peril in *Appointment with Danger* starring Alan Ladd. Dan Dailey and Anne Baxter put on their dancing shoes for musical *You're My Everything*. Dana Andrews romanced Susan Hayward in *My Foolish Heart*, Bing Crosby the star turn in horse racing drama *Riding High*, Myrna Loy and Clifton Webb hapless parents in comedy *Cheaper by the Dozen* and Barbara Stanwyck a blackmail victim in *No Man of Her Own*. Film noir *Night and the City* was directed by Jules Dassin and featured Richard Widmark

JOAN OF ARC

starring INGRID

BERGMAN

A VICTOR FLEMING PRODUCTION

Produced by WALTER WANGER

Directed by VICTOR FLEMING

Based on the Stage Play "JOAN of LORRAINE" by MAXWELL ANDERSON

Color By TECHNICOLOR

A CAST OF THOUSANDS

with JOSE FERRER

FRANCIS L. SULLIVAN · J. CARROL NAISH · WARD BOND

SHEPPERD STRUDWICK · HURD HATFIELD · GENE LOCKHART

JOHN EMERY · GEORGE COULOURIS · JOHN IRELAND and CECIL KELLAWAY

Screenplay by MAXWELL ANDERSON and ANDREW SOLT · Art Direction by RICHARD DAY

Director of Photography JOSEPH VALENTINE, A.S.C.

Presented by SIERRA PICTURES, INC. · Released by RKO RADIO PICTURES

Ingrid Bergman was nominated for an Oscar for *Joan of Arc*, her fourth nomination in six years. She won for *Gaslight* (1944).

53

and Gene Tierney. Rising star Montgomery Clift was in *The Big Lift*. Poisoned Edmond O'Brien had only a few days to find out who was trying to kill him in film noir *D.O.A* while Richard Widmark raced against time in Elia Kazan's *Panic in the Streets*. Betty Grable was the main attraction of musical *Wabash Avenue* and Orson Welles an uncredited director on historical adventure *Black Magic*, in which he also starred, while Delmer Daves' western *Broken Arrow* starring James Stewart set a new tone for the genre.

What the Public Wanted .

In general terms, Paisley cinemagoers responded most often to comedies. But laughter was not an out-and-out winner. It was closely followed by crime – comprising both film noir and gangster pictures – and dramas. It was a relatively close-run thing between the three genres: comedy, which included films with songs but not mainstream musicals, accounted for the largest proportion of films on offer with 24 per cent of the total. Crime was not far behind on 22 percent with drama next on 21 per cent. Surprisingly, westerns, considered one of the dominant genres in the 1950s, accounted for just over 12 percent, with musicals, war, documentary and animation filling in the rest.

However, other distinctions began to emerge when the data was interrogated from a different perspective. More dramas were shown as main features or single bills rather than supports and the same was true of the crime/thriller category. However, it was the opposite for westerns, with films of that nature more likely to be found on the lower end of a double bill. In one way these differences were easily explained; but in another they were not. Westerns had always been a B-movie staple and so were often made with the express intention of filling a spot in a programme rather than being the main attraction. B-films worked to very tight budgets because generally they were sold to cinemas for a fixed sum rather than a share of the ticket sales. What was most important for a B-film was to get into as many cinemas as possible rather than to get into the best or biggest houses. Yet crime films were also equally churned out to meet the demands of the B-film market, most often in series films like Charlie Chan or Bulldog Drummond. So what happened to make crime films make the jump into single bill status or to become the top film in a double bill?

What happened was the boom in film noir which was essentially a new genre, the classic period of this type of film considered to have been kicked off by *The Maltese Falcon* in 1941 and owing much to the social upheavals of the Second World War and the explosion of a gangster "class" in the 1930s. The films had their own heroes and, in many cases, anti-heroes, and often women, rather than being stout upholders of morality, would turn out to be the villains. And the movies had their own particular styles, the black-and-white idiom of the 1940s lending itself to light falling in a particular way, particularly through windows, and bars (windows, staircases etc) serving to hem in the characters. As the genre grew more popular and expanded into the mainstream likes of *Mildred Pierce* (1945) starring Joan Crawford, Gene Tierney as *Laura* (1945) and Rita Hayworth as *Gilda* (1946), the crime picture moved out of the shadows of B-film production and into the mainstream with bigger budgets and stars and from there they were obvious candidates for single-bill or top-of-the-bill treatment in cinemas.

Westerns, on the other hand, had struggled to move solidly into the mainstream. It has to be remembered, in any discussion of this genre, that it, too, was a relatively recent development. Although westerns had always existed in abundance from the early silent period onwards, they were primarily of the small-budget series type with a repeating character engaged in much the same activity in each successive picture. The first trend towards bigger budgets and a more prestigious approach came with the *Big Trail* (1930) starring John Wayne and *Cimarron* (1931) based on the Edna Ferber bestseller. But they could not have achieved more opposite outcomes. The former was a big flop and killed off any chance of John Wayne moving from B-pictures to A-pictures for the best part of a decade while the latter was a hit and took home the Best Picture Oscar. Even so, this type of picture sat uneasily with audiences until the emergence of singing cowboys Roy Rogers and Gene Autry in the mid 1930s. Since these movies regularly made ten times their miserly budgets, often as low as $50,000 at a time when top Hollywood features cost $2-$3million, there was little onus on the major studios to develop the genre. However, following the trend for historical adventure films which required the use of locations, the western sprang almost fully-formed into existence in 1939 with the unveiling of John Ford's *Stagecoach* starring Claire Trevor (John Wayne was not the star, being billed third), Cecil B DeMille's *Union Pacific* starring Barbara Stanwyck and Joel McCrea, Henry King's *Jesse James* starring Tyrone Power and Henry Fonda, and Michael Curtiz's *Dodge City* starring Errol Flynn and Olivia de Havilland.

Above: popular reissue *Jesse James* (1939) directed by Henry King.

After this exhilarating restart, however, the genre fell apart after the United States entered the Second World War in 1941 and although output of the B-movies remained steady the bigger features that attracted top directors and stars went into disrepair. The situation was only revived post-war and in haphazard fashion, John Ford leading the way with *My Darling Clementine* (1946) starring Henry Fonda, *Fort Apache* (1948) and *She Wore a Yellow Ribbon* (1949), both starring John Wayne, Howard Hawks contributing a debut western *Red River* (1948) with John Wayne and newcomer Montgomery Clift, plus William Wellman's *Yellow Sky* (1948) with Gregory Peck who also co-starred with Jennifer Jones in *Duel in the Sun* (1946). But, still, the genre was mostly littered with B-movies and it was noticeable that only one western (*Broken Arrow*) qualified for the accolade of being shown in a single bill in Paisley in 1950.

The figures told their own story. While 67 percent of the dramas were shown as main features and 53 percent of the crime/thrillers, only 46 per cent of the westerns were the main attraction. However, westerns enjoyed the longest runs, an average of 4.54 days per picture, compared to 4.22 days for dramas and 4.17 days for crime-thrillers.

What the Public Did Not Want

Although cinema receipts are generally taken together as an amalgam of a country, it is also the case that a movie does better in some parts of the country than others. Over the years cinema managers would acquire knowledge of audience preference and would ensure that films were not booked to which the local public displayed a clear aversion. In the case of Paisley this was British films. It is well-known that this antipathy towards what were seen as "English" films was shared by the rest of Scotland. This has generally been put down to the fact that most of the country was working-class and that the dislike was based on an aversion to hearing upper-class voices invading their lives. It would be worth discovering whether audiences in other typical working class cities in England itself, such as Newcastle or Liverpool, held the same views. However, what is rarely taken into account is that Scotland has, historically, enjoyed the largest density of cinemagoing audiences and that the level, per head of population, of people attending the cinema on a regular basis outstripped everywhere except London. The frequent filmgoer is bound to be more choosy, and more knowledgeable, than one who goes less often. It is entirely possible that Paisley filmgoers based their dislike of British films on the basis of their understanding and appreciation of the better quality of Hollywood films, which they deemed to have higher production values, bigger stars, more pace and more relevant and realistic stories.

In the context of this pronounced preference, it is worth noting how strong it actually was. Out of 1,255 films shown in 1950 in Paisley only 109 (less than nine per

59

cent) were British. Put another way, over 90 per cent of the movies released in Paisley were not British. Even films like Ealing comedy *Whisky Galore* and POW war picture *The Wooden Horse* (which was given the exceptionally rare marketing accolade of being advertised in the local paper) only ran for three days apiece. *The Third Man*, with a British director but American stars and the recipient of many awards, possibly received its greatest accolade in Paisley when it was only one of two British films that year to be shown over 12 days, the other being Anna Neagle in *Maytime in Mayfair*.

However, of the British films seen in Paisley in 1950, 71 per cent were top of the double bill. Technically, *Treasure Island*, the film given the widest initial release was a British film, but with the backing of Walt Disney it had a more substantial production budget than most British films. Apart from that and *The Third Man* and *Maytime in Mayfair,* in terms of initial release the best performing films were each shown as the main feature in a double bill for a total of six days. Some of these movies featured actors and actresses who would later go on to bigger things in Britain and America but were either at the beginnings of their careers or did not prove to have sufficient pulling power.

Crime was as much a mainstay of British film production as it was in Hollywood and into this category fell embezzlement drama *A Matter of Murder* with Maureen Riscoe and John Barry, *Dark Secret* featured Dinah Sheridan and *The Hidden Room* with Robert Newton. Set in a Borstal institution for young offenders, *The Boys in Brown* had a strong cast headed by Jack Warner (*The Blue Lamp*), Richard Attenborough, who had shot to fame in *Brighton Rock* (1948), and Dirk Bogarde in his fifth movie. The pressures of living in the notorious Glasgow slum almost drive an artist to murder in *The Gorbals Story*. Nominated for a Best Film Bafta, post-war romantic thriller *The Great Manhunt* had a top-notch cast in the shape of Douglas Fairbanks Jr., Glynis Johns and Jack Hawkins. Alistair Sim and Margaret Rutherford clashed in the school-based comedy *The Happiest Days of Your Life*, a big hit elsewhere in the country and a precursor to the St Trinian's sagas. Children were at the heart of the narratives for *No Place for Jennifer* starring Leo Genn and the adaptation of the D.H. Lawrence short story *The Rocking Horse Winner* starring Valerie Hobson. Jean Simmons, already in the Hollywood sights after David Lean's *Great Expectations* (1946) and *The Blue Lagoon* (1948), and Dirk Bogarde toplined psychological thriller *So Long at the Fair*.

Less well-known actors were the stars of war film *They Were Not Divided* (Edward Underdown), comedy *Up for the Cup* (Arthur Modley) and *The Chiltern Hundreds* (Gladys Boot). But war drama *Landfall* was directed by Ken Annakin (*The Longest Day*), based on a Nevil Shute bestseller and featured Michael Dennison. Terence Fisher directed *Marry Me*, a comedy about a marriage bureau with Derek Bond and Susan Shaw. Michael Rennie and Yolande Donlan headed up the Val Guest comedy *Miss*

Pilgrim's Progress. A train disaster shown from four different perspectives formed the crux of *Train of Events* also starring Jack Warner. Arthur Lucan and Kitty McShane reprised the roles they had been playing since 1937 in the series film *Old Mother Riley's New Venture*.

Films getting minimal exposure, just three days top of the bill, and, therefore, effectively, disdained by the Paisley film bookers included David Lean's *Madeleine* starring Ann Todd and based on a famous Glasgow murder case in 1857 and Alec Guinness in *The Last Holiday. The Golden Salamander*, from the Victor Canning thriller, starred Trevor Howard, one of the country's biggest stars after *Brief Encounter* (1945). *Dance Hall*, directed by Ealing stalwart Charles Crichton, followed the tribulations of four factory girls including Jane Hylton and Diana Dors. David Farrar, another strong attraction, as well as Honor Blackman and Diana Dors, was in *Diamond City*, an adventure set in the South African diamond mines. Glaswegian Gordon Jackson took the lead in shipbuilding drama *Floodtide*, also starring Edinburgh actress Rona Anderson. Psychological thriller *Guilt Is My Shadow* starred Peter Reynolds and Elizabeth Sellars while crime drama *Interrupted Journey* had Valerie Hobson and Richard Todd heading the cast.

Series and Serials

With less interest than might be expected in the output of the British film industry, and demand for programmes still high, cinema managers had to call upon other sources of material. Luckily, there were any number of low-budget pictures and B-movies available. Many of these were what were known as "series" films where an actor played the same character in every film.

These ranged from westerns featuring series characters Hopalong Cassidy, The Cisco Kid, Red Ryder and singing cowboys Roy Rogers and Gene Autry, to detectives Sherlock Holmes, Charlie Chan and Nero Wolfe, comedic turns such as Jiggs and Maggie, Ma and Pa Kettle, Blondie and Britain's own contribution to the sub-genre Old Mother Riley, crime dramas/comedies The Bowery Boys and The East Side Kids, and bigger-budgeted jungle adventures featuring Tarzan and Jungle Jim.

Although held in low esteem by the critics, the series films performed a vital function in filling out programmes. In total the series pictures accounted for almost 300 days of programming in Paisley in 1950. Westerns featuring the likes of Hopalong Cassidy, Roy Rogers and Gene Autry had the faithful support of millions of fans. Rogers was especially popular in Scotland because of his Scottish ancestry and his highly-publicised love of poet Robert Burns.

Top: William Boyd as Hopalong Cassidy. Below: the East Side Kids were a B-film staple.

The screen's ORIGINAL toughies in a rip-roaring story from the *Saturday Evening Post!*

THE
EAST SIDE KIDS...
"KID DYNAMITE"

Leo GORCEY
Bobby JORDAN
Huntz HALL
Gabriel DELL
Featuring Pamela Blake

THEY CAN'T
BE TOPPED!

When Those Bowery Bombers Start Fighting Among Themselves ... You're In for a Big Barrage of Thrills!

• • •

DYNAMITE
At Any Box-Office!

Book The East Side Kids
from
MONOGRAM

ATLANTA • CHARLOTTE • OKLAHOMA CITY
MEMPHIS • NEW ORLEANS • DALLAS

Gene Autry and detectives like Sherlock Holmes are the best-known today of the old series characters, the most popular series star in 1950 in Paisley was Leo Gorcey who single-handedly accounted for 50 days of screen time through 11 pictures, four of which (*Trouble Makers, Bowery Champs, Kid Dynamite* and *Spooks Run Wild*) were presented as main features, with two crime series in play, The Bowery Boys and The East Side Kids. William Boyd as Hopalong Cassidy also had 11 pictures doing the rounds in 1950, occupying 38 days in cinemas, the most popular being *Sinister Journey, Strange Gamble, Borrowed Trouble* and *The Devil's Playground* but all his films were supports. Johnny "Mack" Brown as Red Ryder enjoyed 35 days from seven films, again all shown as supports. Charlie Chan aficionados had the opportunity to compare two previous interpretations of the sleuth – Warner Roland in *Charlie Chan at Monte Carlo* (1937) and Sidney Toler in *Charlie Chan in Reno* (1939) and *Dead Men Tell* (1941) - with that of the present incumbent Roland Winters who could be seen in *The Feathered Serpent* (1948), *Golden Eye* (1948) and *Shanghai Chest* (1948). All told the six movies ran for 26 days. Johnny Weissmuller did double duty as Tarzan (*Tarzan and the Mermaids*) and Jungle Jim (*Jungle Jim, The Mark of the Gorilla* and *The Lost Tribe*), all main attractions, which racked up 24 days.

The films of Roy Rogers were so simplistic that to save audiences the trouble of having to work out who the star played in each individual film the producers simply called

65

the characters after the name of the star. Although he did not have as many films in view as some of his series competitors, Rogers was actually a bigger star than most, since four films out of five – *Down Dakota Way*, *The Gay Ranchero*, *Springtime in the Sierras* and *Under Californian Skies* - went out as the main feature on a double bill for a total of 23 days playing time. Duncan Renaldo's four outings as The Cisco Kid clocked up 21 days. Penny Singleton, as Blondie, was another whose films, five in 1950, appeared as supports, for 18 days. Gene Autry's approach was similar to that of Roy Rogers not just that he played himself in all his movies but as an attraction whose films were top-billed, the 1950 trio of *Saddle Pals*, *Loaded Pistols* and *The Last Round Up* marking up 11 days on the screens.

Other series characters who put in an appearance included former "Falcon" Tom Conway as Bulldog Drummond in *The Challenge* (1948) and *13 Lead Soldiers* (1948), Basil Rathbone as Sherlock Holmes in *Pursuit to Algiers* (1945), Morris Chester in *Boston Blackie's Chinese Venture* (1949), John Calvert as The Falcon in *Appointment with Murder* (1948) and *Search for Danger* (1949) and Walter Connolly as Nero Wolfe in *The League of Frightened Men* (1937). *The Notorious Lone Wolf* (1946) played by Gerald Mohr could be compared to *The Lone Wolf and the Lady* (1949) with Ron Randell doing the honours. Marjorie Main and Percy Kilbride as *Ma and Pa Kettle* (1949) was quickly followed by *Ma and Pa Kettle Go to Town* (1950), the first a main feature, the

66

second a support, both given only three days. The Jiggs and Maggie series were based on comic strip characters played by Joe Yule and Renie Riano. The series had made its debut in 1947 and the next two pictures *Jiggs and Maggie in Court* (1948) and *Jiggs and Maggie in Jackpot Jitters* (1949) turned up in Paisley in 1950, both as supports, the first running for six days, the second for nine.

"Old Mother Riley" had been a British film institution since 1937 with Irish comedian Arthur Lucan in drag playing the titular character and his real-life wife Kitty McShane her/his daughter, but in fact the characters had their origins in a music hall act. Their movies appeared at the rate of one or two a year, although there were none in 1942 and three in 1943. The series was so successful that Lucan made the Top Ten of British movie stars in 1942. There had been twelve in the series so far and in 1950 Paisley played host to a retread of *Old Mother Riley's Circus* (1941), which appeared as a support, as well as the latest in the series *Old Mother Riley's New Venture* (1949) which was deemed worthy of being a main feature.

While the heyday of the serial was long gone, two cinemas in particular, the West End and the New Alex, had found continued demand for them. So much so that they put a great deal of marketing punch behind their launch, far more than they invested in any ordinary picture. Prior to the beginning of any serial, the two cinemas would run advertisements on the front page of the *Paisley Daily Express* and inside. The serials were seen as

Ralph Byrd as Dick Tracy was also a TV series in 1950.

an added incentive to attract cinemagoers and only shown in the second half of the week, on Thu-Sat, with one episode being screened every week. None of the serials were new, since the fashion for them had long since abated. The 13-episode *Flash Gordon*, based on the Alex Raymond comic strip and starring Buster Crabbe, dated back to 1936. Each episode lasted just over 18 minutes, but Universal had put a hefty budget ($360,000) behind the production. Republic had launched the 15-episode *Dick Tracy*, also based on a comic strip (by Chester Gould) and starring Ralph Byrd in 1937. *Dick Tracy Returns* had been originally released in 1938. The most recent serial *The Purple Monster Strikes*, a sci-fi actioner, made by Republic in 1945, and starred Dennis Moore.

68

Reissues

With only just over a hundred of the movies released in Paisley in 1950 originating in that year, it stood to reason that over 90 per cent of the films available were made previously. Quite how far back in the Hollywood inventory cinemas were willing to go to fill their programmes and Paisley's reliance on reissues was one of the unusual findings of this research. Some oldies were being shown again for the umpteenth time, others plucked from the catalogue on a one-off basis, while a significant number were the subject of a concerted reissue following the post-war boom in revivals in the U.S., when several movies – *A Rage in Heaven* (MGM, 1941) for example - made more at the box office than on initial release.

The oldest movie on show in 1950 dated back to 1931: Laurel and Hardy in *Jailbirds* (aka *Pardon Us*). Other Stan and Ollie oldies from this decade also screened during this year included *Pack up Your Troubles* (1932), *Wooden Soldiers* aka *Babes in Toyland* (1934), *Our Relations* (1936) and *Jitterbugs* (1936). Harold Lloyd in *Movie Crazy* (1932) also aired, as did, from the same year, James Cagney in *Winner Take All*. The quality of the oldies varied considerably. There was no doubting the vintage of William Wyler's *Dead End* (1937) starring James Cagney and Humphrey Bogart, Marlene Dietrich and James Stewart in *Destry Rides Again* (1939), Gary Cooper in *The Lives of a Bengal Lancer* (1936), Cary Grant and Joan Fontaine in *Gunga Din* (1939), Sabu in Alexander Korda's *Drum* (1938), Ingrid Bergman in her

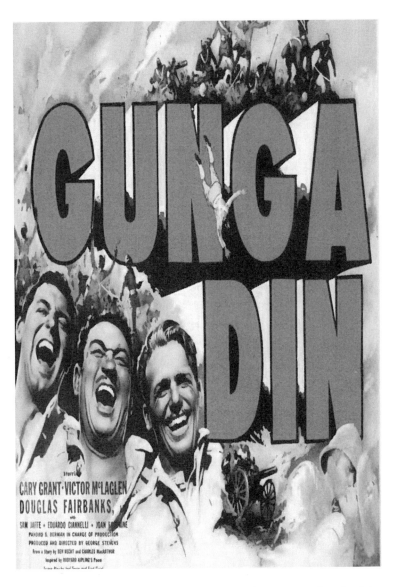

Above: Ten writers, including William Faulkner, were involved in bringing the Rudyard Kipling poem *Gunga Din* to the screen.

Above: Ida Lupino was so popular that cinemas reprised *One Rainy Afternoon* from 1936.

Hollywood debut *Escape to Happiness* aka *Intermezzo* (1939) and Tyrone Power as *Jesse James* (1939). Also entering the frame were Fred Astaire and Ginger Rogers in *Top Hat* (1935), Edward G. Robinson and Jean Arthur in *Passport to Fame* (1935), Randolph Scott in *The Last of the Mohicans* (1936), Ida Lupino in *The Gay Desperado* (1936) and *One Rainy Afternoon* (1936), Tyrone Power as *Jesse James* (1939), Lon Chaney in *Destiny* (aka *The Wolf Man*, 1939), Bob Hope in *Some Like it Hot* (1939), Loretta Young in *Kentucky* (1938), Brian Aherne and Victor McLaglen in *Captain Fury* (1939), and John Ford's *Stagecoach* (1939).

From the first half of the 1940s came Gary Cooper in *John Doe Dynamite* (aka *Meet John Doe*, 1941) and *The Pride of the Yankees* (1942), Alfred Hitchcock's *Rebecca* (1940), *Kit Carson* (1940), *Bad Men of Missouri* (1941), Abbott and Costello in *Who Done It?* (1942) and *Lost in a Harem* (1944), John Wayne in *Dark Command* (1940) and *Flying Tigers* (1942), Ingrid Bergman in *Adam Had Four Sons* (1941), Betty Grable in musical *Down Argentine Way* (1940) and Lana Turner and Joan Blondell in *Choose Your Partner* (1940).

But the regiment of reissues was also flooded with B-movies such as *Charlie Chan in Monte Carlo* (1937) and *Charlie Chan in Reno* (1939). The earliest of The East Side Kids pictures dated back to 1943 – *Kid Dynamite* and *The Clancy Street Boys* - while *The Bowery at Midnight* first saw light of day in 1942 and *Bowery Champs* in 1944. There were also a number of oddities (in terms of

72

becoming candidates for revival) such as David Niven in *Dinner at the Ritz* (1937), Jean Arthur in *Diamond Jim* (1935) and Lynn Bari in *Chasing Danger* (1939). In exploiting the potential of the series films, cinemas invariably dug into the studio archives, Laurel and Hardy, for example, having 11 films hitting the screens, virtually all supporting features, *Bohemian Girl* (1936) the exception, but still credited with a total of 44 days' worth of screenings.

Below: Marjorie Main, of "Ma and Pa Kettle" fame was an added attraction in the re-release of *Dark Command*.

Foreign Films

Augmenting the supply of new films were a half-dozen movies from abroad, split equally between Australia and Italy. The first of the three Australian films to turn up in Paisley (in May 1950) was horse racing drama *Into the Straight* starring Shirley Hall and Margo Lee.

Filmed on location in Sydney, Victoria and Scone in New South Wales, it was made by Australian outfit Embassy and picked up for distribution by Universal, but was relegated to a support in one cinema for three days. Next up (June 1950) was war film *The Rats of Tobruk* (aka *The Fighting Rats of Tobruk*), made by Chamum Productions and filmed at the Commonwealth Film Laboratories in New South Wales.

It was six years old by the time it was unveiled in Paisley as a supporting feature. In retrospect it had a distinguished cast, Chips Rafferty who would become a major star in his home country and Peter Finch (*Network*) who would win acclaim in Britain and Hollywood. Lastly (November 1950), came *The Rugged Riordans*, the story of five brothers who battled the Australian bush to set up a farm, a co-production between Australian distributor Greater Union Organisation and Universal and starred Michael Pate and Jen Wayne.

This was shown for three days in two cinemas, in one picture house as the main feature and in the other as the support.

The Golden Madonna (1949) was an Italian-British co-production. The film was produced by Produttore Films International in conjunction with Independent Film Producers and Pendennis Productions with two directors – Italian Luigi Carpentieri and Hungarian Ladislao Vadja. British stars Phyllis Calvert and Michael Rennie took the leading roles but most of the supporting cast were Italian. The five writers involved, including Glaswegian Aimee Stuart, Hungarian Akos Tolnay (also a co-producer) and Italian Bruno Valneri, cooked up a tale about the hunt for a lost painting. The crew were Italian.

The British print was edited down by six minutes from the Italian 94-minute version. The movie was shown as a main feature for three days in one cinema.

Prelude to Fame (1950) was another Italian-British co-production, this time with Two Cities Films (*Henry V*, 1945, and *Hamlet*, 1948) teaming up with Aquila Cinematografica. Based on an Aldous Huxley short story *Young Archimedes*, the entire cast was British, top roles taken by Guy Rolfe and Kathleen Byron, who had appeared in the Powell/Pressburger dramas *Black Narcissus* (1947) and *A Matter of Life and Death* (1946). It was the second film of director Fergus McDonell after *The Hideout* (1948). It was shot on location in Florence and Naples and in Pinewood Studios. However, it had a truncated release in Paisley, only managing one three-day booking and even then as a support.

After the Italian-made *Stromboli* (above), Ingrid Bergman did not make another movie in Hollywood for six years. By then she was clearly forgiven, winning the Oscar for *Anastasia* (1956).

An Italian co-production with RKO, *Stromboli* was one of the the most sensational movies to come out of Europe, mostly because of the scandal surrounding the affair between Ingrid Bergman and Italian director Roberto Rossellini, a married man.

By comparison, comedy *A Night of Fame* (1949) was the genuine original Italian article. The film's star was French boxer Marcel Cerdan supported by Italian Ferruccio Tagliavini, Russian Mischa Auer and American Marilyn Buferd as the girl for whom three men are willing to trade their souls to the Devil, but the rest of the cast was primarily Italian. The film was directed by Italians Mario Monicelli and Steno (making his debut), both of whom had a hand in the script, made by Produttori Associati, and distributed in the UK by independent D.U.K. In Paisley it ran for six days as a main feature.

Chapter Three: The Top Stars

We are perhaps conditioned to believe that in the 1950s movie stars dominated the lives of ordinary people, that the general public envied their grand homes, families and lifestyles, and, of course, reacted to detrimental news coverage of marriage break-ups or divorces. While these aspects of Hollywood might have been reflected in the more popular national daily newspapers, they were never touched upon within the confines of a local newspaper of this period, if the *Paisley Daily Express* is anything to go by. However, the exact extent of movie star worship is open to question. Hollywood producers or agents were hardly roaming the streets of Paisley on the off-chance of finding a potential new star sitting in a tearoom, so one element of the Hollywood Dream was a non-starter in Scotland. But worship depends, as much as anything, on access. As this survey shows, not all the big stars were big in Paisley – and I wonder how much Paisley was reflective of the rest of the country outside of the big city cinemas. Although actors made movies at the rate of two or three a year, their pictures might only play for three days in one cinema in an entire year, an action that was hardly likely to increase their popularity.

While cinemas had to fall in line to screen new pictures, the oldies of the bigger stars were more readily available and often were screened precisely because the star was involved in a current success. The smaller cinemas in

Paisley would often show a two- or three-day run of an older film featuring an actor or actress currently enjoying a six-day run at one of the plusher theaters. In addition, when actors suddenly became famous, movies in which they had previously starred but had not received a particular push at the box office could be sharply brought in to cash in on their newfound fame, as seen with Virginia Mayo and Alexis Smith. However, a cinema manager was instrumental in building or sustaining that popularity. By scheduling the films of a particular star, a manager would provide fans with greater access to a star. And, of course, the opposite held true. In this fashion, popularity is relatively easy to measure. Local appreciation of a star can easily be gauged by the number of days and/or cinemas in which his/her movies played, and by how often these movies returned either in the form of quick repeats or as revivals of earlier movies.

Paisley's Number One Star: Virginia Mayo

Using this technique, the top draw in 1950 in Paisley was, rather surprisingly, screen beauty **Virginia Mayo**. She had overcome early rejection – talent spotted by MGM and screen tested by David O. Selznick but not given any parts – before being signed by independent producer Samuel Goldwyn who nursed her career until at the age of 24, in her third movie role, she played the leading lady opposite Bob Hope in the comedy *Princess and the Pirate* (1944). She polished her acting credentials in the Oscar-winning

The Best Years of Our Lives (1946) as the unfaithful wife of star Dana Andrews and turned up the heat on her comic talent as the nightclub singer being wooed by Danny Kaye in *The Kid from Brooklyn* (1946). From then on, her status as a leading lady continued to rise until she won top billing in her own right virtually immediately with mystery thriller *Smart Girls Don't Talk* (1947) and thereafter alternated roles in which she was the undisputed lead with acting as the leading lady to comedy or singing stars. She re-teamed with Kaye on *The Secret Life of Walter Mitty* (1947) and *A Song Is Born* (1948) and, in a complete change of pace, made an explosive appearance in Howard Hawks' gangster sizzler *White Heat* (1949) starring James Cagney.

The true definition of a star was that cinemas clamoured not just for their most recent pictures but for anything that had come before, and, in this regard, Paisley was well served by Virginia Mayo. In 1950, eight of her movies were shown in the town, running for a total of 53 days. Her hit octet, in a diversity of roles in a variety of genres, were: *The Secret Life of Walter Mitty, Smart Girls Don't Talk, A Song Is Born,* comedy *Always Leave 'Em Laughing* (1949), film noir *Flaxy Martin* (1949), *White Heat,* Raoul Walsh western *Colorado Territory* (1949) and romantic comedy *The Girl from Jones Beach* (1949) with Ronald Reagan.

MILTON
BERLE

VIRGINIA
MAYO

"ALWAYS LEAVE
THEM LAUGHING"

Milton Berle had made his movie debut in *The Perils of Pauline* in
1914.

The Rest of the Paisley Top Ten

Runner-ups jointly were comedy duo **Abbott & Costello** (12 films, 47 days) and **John Wayne** (13 films, 47 days). Perhaps the most difficult aspect of getting a proper grip on the past is avoiding the trap of viewing it from a historical perspective. Unlike Laurel and Hardy, the Marx Brothers and Harold Lloyd, the works of Bud Abbott and Lou Costello have not held up so well for succeeding generations and, consequently, they have not only fallen down the roster in the Hollywood Comedy Hall of Fame but virtually off the radar as well. However, in their day, they were extremely popular, with pictures regularly among the highest-earning at the box office and hugely appreciated all over the world including small towns like Paisley. They belonged to the 1930s generation – Bob Hope, Bing Crosby and Red Skelton being others – who made an effortless transition from radio to the big screen, but, in that respect, were late bloomers making their Hollywood debut, and not in the leading roles, in 1940 in *One Night in the Tropics*. In their next picture, *Buck Privates*, they were top billed and went from strength to strength, churning out 15 movies in the next five years. By the end of the decade, the formula was somewhat diluted, as were the box office returns, and by then they had spoofed virtually every genre from war films and westerns to horror and jungle adventure. The two most recent pictures in their oeuvre - *Africa Screams* (1949) and *Abbot and Costello Meet the Killer, Boris Karloff* (1949) - were both considered strong enough for main features

Abbott and Costello had made their name in radio so it was perhaps fitting that *Who Done It* (1942) was set in a radio station.

in Paisley in 1950. But so were another ten of their comedies: *Ride Em Cowboy* (1942), *Who Done It?* (1942) *Hit the Ice* (1943), *Lost in a Harem* (1944), *Abbott and Costello Meet the Coeds* (1945), *The Naughty Nineties* (1945), *The Wistful Widow of Wagon Gap* (1947), *The*

83

Noose Hangs High (1948), *Mexican Hayride* (1948), and *Abbott and Costello Meet the Ghosts* (1948),

John Wayne was equally as interesting a figure from the historical perspective. At this point in his career, he was only a few years into being accepted as bona fide top-of-the-bill leading man. Even after his breakthrough in John Ford's *Stagecoach* (1939), where he received third billing, he took second billing for most of the early-to-mid-1940s, behind Claire Trevor in *Allegheny Uprising* (1940) and *Dark Command* (1940), behind Marlene Dietrich in *Seven Sinners* (1940), *The Spoilers* (1942) and *Pittsburgh* (1942), behind Joan Blondell in *Lady for a Night* (1942), behind Ray Milland in Cecil B. DeMille's *Reap the Wild Wind* (1942), behind Joan Crawford in *Reunion in France* (1942), behind Jean Arthur in *Lady Takes a Chance* (1943), behind Robert Montgomery in John Ford war film *They Were Expendable* (1945), and even as late as 1946 below Claudette Colbert in the billing for *Without Reservations*. However, the fact that he had a full back catalogue meant that it could be plundered at will by cinema owners and for those films where he had technically not been star a slight readjustment on the poster could make it look as though he was. A dozen John Waynes made pit stops in Paisley in 1950, though mostly in three-day slots. Two films were each shown three times in different cinemas. His most recent pictures were adventure *The Fighting Kentuckian* (1949) and the second of the John Ford 'Cavalry' trilogy *She Wore a Yellow Ribbon* (1949). The other ten pictures doing the rounds

84

Top: John Wayne was not the original star of *They Were Expendable*. Bottom: He was the star of *Wake of the Red Witch*.

were: *Stagecoach*, Republic B-western *New Frontier* (1939), Raoul Walsh historical drama *Dark Command*, war film *Flying Tigers* (1942), drama *Flame of the Barbary Coast* (1945) with Ann Dvorak, war films *Back to Bataan* (1945) and *They Were Expendable* (1945), romantic comedy *Without Reservations*, Howard Hawks western *Red River* (1948), adventure *Wake of the Red Witch* (1948), and *The Three Godfathers* (1948). Although still shy of the biggest 1950s hits of his career – *The Sands of Iwo Jima*, *The Quiet Man* and *The Searchers* – and although none of the films shown in 1950 in Paisley had been (with the exception of *Stagecoach*, *Reap the Wild Wind* and *Red River*) huge hits, there was clearly enormous support for the actor at ground level, otherwise cinema managers would not have programmed so many of his oldies.

In fourth spot in the Top Ten was another unexpected figure - **Alexis Smith** – who had eight films on screens for a total of 46 days. From today's perspective, she is largely a forgotten actress but, like Abbott and Costello, was a prominent personality of the period. Promoted, to her annoyance, as the "Dynamite Girl", she had made her screen debut as the leading lady in *Dive Bomber* (1941) starring Errol Flynn and teamed up with him again the following year in boxing biopic *Gentleman Jim* and thereafter played opposite most of the top males including Humphrey Bogart and Clark Gable and received excellent reviews for her performance as *The Constant Nymph* (1943) opposite Charles Boyer and in Michael Curtiz's biopic *Night and Day* (1946) as the wife of Cole Porter played by Cary Grant. Again, there were enough of her films in the vaults to keep her fans satisfied. The eight films taking root in Paisley in 1950 were: Raoul Walsh musical comedy *Young Man with a Horn* (1945) with Jack

Benny, a third outing with Flynn in western *San Antonio* (1945), divorce drama *The Decision of Christopher Blake* (1948), film noir *Whiplash* (1948), romantic comedy *One Last Fling* (1949), war drama *Any Number Can Play* (1949) opposite Gable, western *South of St Louis* (1949) and another teaming with Flynn in *Montana* (1950).

Humphrey Bogart was joint fifth alongside Hollywood heavyweight **Errol Flynn** and newcomer **Van Johnson** who had seven movies apiece each playing the same number of days: 41. Swashbuckler Flynn was an unusual choice to team up with top British star Greer Garson for *The Forsyte Saga* (aka *That Forsyte Woman*, 1949) especially given the distance between them in terms of critical accolades. Garson had been nominated for the Oscar for five years in a row from 1942 to 1946, winning the statuette for *Mrs Miniver* (1942), whereas the closest Flynn had come to any recognition was twice receiving the Sour Apple Award for the least cooperative actor in the eyes of the media. However, the teaming proved popular with British audiences and revived interest in the fading Hollywood star. Apart from *The New Adventures of Don Juan* (1948) with Viveca Lindfors, the star had turned more recently to westerns. In Paisley in 1950 Flynn could be seen in western revival *San Antonio* (1945), mystery *Cry Wolf* (1947) with Barbara Stanwyck, drama *Escape Me Never* (1947) with Ida Lupino, *The New Adventures of Don Juan*s, Raoul Walsh western *Silver River* (1948) with Ann Sheridan, and western *Montana* (1950).

87

Bogart's magnificent seven were: *Crime's End*, previously known as *Dead End* (1937), *Crime School* (1938), Howard Hawks private eye flick *The Big Sleep* (1946), John Huston crime drama *Key Largo* (1948) with Lauren Bacall, Huston's hymn to greed *The Treasure of the Sierra Madre* (1948), war picture *Tokyo Joe* (1948), Nicholas Ray's *Knock on Any Door* (1949), film noir *In a Lonely Place* (1950) with Gloria Grahame and aviation spectacle *Chain Lightning* (1950) with Eleanor Parker.

Van Johnson was the new kid on the block, MGM's latest sensation. He had made his debut in low-budget prison drama *Murder in the Big House* (1942) before graduating to MGM's *A Guy Named Joe* with third billing behind Spencer Tracy and Irene Dunne following up the next year with his first starring role in a big budget film *Two Girls and a Sailor*. He quickly became a matinee idol and when magazines put his picture on the cover they soon sold out. He should have been a musical star, one rung below the likes of Frank Sinatra and Fred Astaire, but his good looks and, more importantly, easy manner provided him with a wider range of roles, and MGM put him centre stage for the first of the great post-war military pictures William Wellman's *Battleground* (1949). His 1950 Paisley septet were: *Between Two Women* (1944), *Two Girls and a Sailor*, war drama *Command Decision* (1949) with Clark Gable, film noir *Scene of the Crime*, and *Mother Knows Best*.

Right: John Huston won Oscars for directing and writing *The Treasure of the Sierra Madre* (1948).

In eighth position was **Barbara Stanwyck**, one of the few silent stars who had successfully made the transition into the talkies, with eight films spread over 40 days – *John Doe Dynamite* (1941), romantic drama *My Reputation* (1946), *Cry Wolf* (1947), Mervyn Leroy romantic drama *East Side West Side* (1949) with British star James Mason, film noir *The Lady Gambles* (1949), Anthony Mann western *The Furies* (1950), film noir *No Man of Her Own* (1950) and Robert Siodmak film noir *The File on Thelma Jordan* (1950).

Rounding out the Top Ten, in joint ninth, were box office stalwart **Gary Cooper** and another newcomer **Ronald Reagan**, the former with eight films totaling 36 days, the latter only needing five to reach the same target. Cooper's pictures ranged from earlier triumphs like Henry Hathaway adventure *The Lives of a Bengal Lancer* (1935), as Wild Bill Hickok in Cecil B. DeMille's *The Plainsman* (1936) and DeMille's *North West Mounted Police* (1940) to Frank Capra's *John Doe Dynamite* aka *Meet John Doe* (1941) and as the afflicted baseball player Lou Gehrig in *The Pride of the Yankees* (1942). The more recent offerings were Leo McCarey romantic comedy *Good Sam* (1948) with Ann Sheridan, Delmer Daves war drama *Task Force* (1949) and as the uncompromising architect in King Vidor's adaptation of the Ayn Rand bestseller *The Fountainhead* (1949).

Barbara Stanwyck had been a star since 1927 when she appeared opposite Rod La Rocque in *The Locked Door.*

By comparison, future U.S. President Reagan's complement of movies were all relatively recent. After making his breakthrough with third billing in Sam Wood's expose *Kings Row* (1942), his career was temporarily truncated by war duty and he did not make another picture until 1947 drama *Stallion Road* with Alexis Smith in which he was top billed. Reagan's oldest picture on show in Paisley in 1950 was romantic comedy *Voice of the Turtle* (1948) with Eleanor Parker, the others being war drama *The Hasty Heart* (1949) with Patricia Neal, comedy *John Loves Mary* (1949), *The Girl from Jones Beach* (1949) with Virginia Mayo and comedy *Louisa* (1950).

Other Stars Making the Paisley Top Thirty

Swedish-born actress **Ingrid Bergman** took 11th spot in the top 20. She appeared in six films, running for 33 days, showing in Paisley in 1950. Two of these were directed by Alfred Hitchcock, the new *Under Capricorn* (1949) and the reissue of *Spellbound* (1945). *Joan of Arc* (1948), one of her other two new pictures, had been produced by her own company. The Italian-made *Stromboli* (1950) was one of the most successful foreign pictures of the year and directed by Roberto Rossellini. During filming, Bergman had fallen in love with the already married Rossellini and created a huge scandal by running off with him, an action that ended with her being boycotted in Hollywood for over a half a decade. Revivals of *Adam Had Four Sons*

(1941) and her Hollywood debut *Escape to Happiness* (aka *Intermezzo*, 1939) completed the half dozen.

Twelfth spot went to **Orson Welles** (five films, 32 days) and **Loretta Young** (seven films, 32 days). Although these days best known for his innovative directing (*Citizen Kane, The Magnificent Ambersons*), Welles had considerable box office appeal as an actor and was currently enjoying his biggest British success in Carol Reed thriller *The Third Man* (1949). He co-starred with Tyrone Power in two adventure pictures, Henry Hathaway's *The Black Rose* (1950) and *Prince of Foxes* (1949). His other pictures were mystery *Black Magic* (1949) and a repeat showing of *Date with Destiny* (aka *The Stranger*, 1946).

Next came **Loretta Young** (six films, 32 days) who had first co-starred with Clark Gable in 1935 for adventure film *Call of the Wild* based on the Jack London novel and 15 years later and now an Oscar-winning actress (for *The Farmer's Daughter*, 1947) the stars were paired again for the comedy *Key to the City* (1950). In addition, Paisley moviegoers were treated in 1950 to her second Oscar nomination for comedy *Come to the Stable* (1949) in which she played a nun. She was also paired with MGM heartthrob Van Johnson for romantic comedy *Mother Knows Best* (aka *Mother Is a Freshman*, 1949). As ever, when demand for a star's films was at its height, cinema managers headed straight for the vaults to revive some of their oldies. In this case, they went   back a few years for

Above: Director Orson Welles (*Citizen Kane*) had become a big office star again in *Black Magic* (1949) after Carol Reed's *The Third Man* (1949) had hit the jackpot.

Date with Destiny (aka *The Stranger*, 1946) in which she shared the screen with Orson Welles and Edward G. Robinson and then back a few more years for sporting drama *Kentucky* (1938) before digging even deeper for *The Honourable Mr Wong* (aka *Hatchet Man*, 1932) in which she had also co-starred with Edward G. Robinson.

Following her came the quintet of **Ida Lupino** (seven films, 31 days), **Joel McCrea** (five films, 31 days), **Denis Morgan** (seven films, 31 days), **George Raft** (five films, 31 days), and **Robert Cummings** (seven films, 31 days). London-born Lupino, one of Warner Brothers' top female stars after heating up the screen in *High Sierra* (1941) with Humphrey Bogart and *The Sea Wolf* (1941) with Edward G. Robinson, had just broken the mould for Hollywood actresses by branching out into screenwriting, producing and directing in *Not Wanted* (1949). Though this last picture had not yet been released in Britain, Lupino proved a top draw through the thriller *Woman in Hiding* (1950) and *Lust for Gold* (1949) with Glenn Ford. But, as we have seen, screen popularity was measured as much by old films as new. Not only had cinema managers pulled out of the archives such previous plums as *Escape Me Never* (1947) with Errol Flynn and the drama *Deep Valley* (1947), they gone back much further for further showings of comedies *The Gay Desperado* (1936) and *One Rainy Afternoon* (1936) and adventure *Let's Get Married* (1937).

At one time a versatile actor handling crime, sophisticated comedy and drama with ease, and at one time Preston

Sturges main choice for leading man (*Sullivan's Travels*, 1941, *The Palm Beach Story*, 1942), by 1950 Joel McCrea's chief calling card was the western. Three of these hit the Paisley screens – *Stars in My Crown* (1950) directed by Jacques Tourneur, Raoul Walsh's *Colorado Territory* (1949) with Virginia Mayo and *South of St Louis* (1949) with Alexis Smith. He also appeared in two revivals – Hitchcock's *Foreign Correspondent* (1940) and William Wyler's *Dead End* (1937).

Dennis Morgan is largely a forgotten Hollywood leading man these days but in the 1940s he was a big Warner Brothers star and, in fact, for most of the decade the studio's highest paid actor. So highly-regarded was he that he was originally offered the part of Rick in *Casablanca*, but turned it down. His biggest hits in Paisley in 1950 were in the dramas *Too Dangerous to Love* (aka *Perfect Stranger*) with Ginger Rogers and *To the Victor* (1948) with Viveca Lindfors; musicals *It's a Great Feeling* (1949) with Doris Day and *One Sunday Afternoon* (1949); and comedy *Two Texas Knights* (1948). He also turned up in revivals of the western *Bad Men of Missouri* (1941) and thriller *Gas Squad* (aka *Tear Gas Squad*, 1940).

George Raft was the archetypal Hollywood tough guy, making his debut in Howard Hawk's gangster classic *Scarface* (1932) and in 1950 there was no sign of those kind of roles drying up. He was seen in a trio of crime pictures: *A Dangerous Profession* (1949), *Hounded* (aka *Johnny Allegro*, 1949) with Nina Foch, and *Race Street* (1948) with William Bendix and Marilyn Maxwell. He also appeared in adventure film *Outpost in Morocco* with Marie Windsor and the revival of *Manpower* (1941) with Edward G. Robinson and Marlene Dietrich and directed by Raoul Walsh.

Robert Cummings was primarily a lightweight comedian (who later had his own U.S. television show, utilising a similar persona, which ran from 1955 to 1959 and then again from 1961 to 1962). Apart from Hitchcock's *The Saboteur* (1942) and *Kings Row* (1942) his acting was strictly on the lighter side of life. However, in 1950, he played against type in the William Dieterle drama *Paid in Full* (1950) up against Lizabeth Scott and as French revolutionary Robespierre in Anthony Mann's historical *Reign of Terror* (1949). Paisley moviegoers had the opportunity to compare those more dramatic performances with his more traditional comedic fare in *Tell it to the Judge* (1949) with Rosalind Russell and *Free For All* (1949) with up-and-coming actress Ann Blyth as well as older lightweight vehicles *Princess O'Rourke* (1943) opposite Olivia De Havilland, *Free and Easy* (1941) and *The Under-Pup* (1939) with Gloria Jean.

Sharing 19th spot were newcomer **Robert Mitchum** and established star **John Payne** (both with eight films, 29 days). John Payne, another forgotten man, was a versatile actor, equally at home in musicals, comedy, adventure thrillers and westerns. He had starred with Betty Grable on radio in the 1930s and he soon found his niche when he was signed up by Twentieth Century Fox in 1940 as the foil to musical stars Alice Faye and Sonja Henie, although his also exercised his dramatic chops opposite Claudette Colbert in weepie *Remember the Day* (1942). His Paisley 1950 portfolio represented all aspects of his talent. There was a western, *The Eagle and the Hawk* (1950) – not to be confused with 1933 aviation film of the same name - with redhead Rhonda Fleming set in Mexico. *Captain China* (1950) with Gail Russell was an action adventure, as was the revived *Wake Up and Dream* (1946). *Crooked Way* (1949) was a thriller while *Sentimental Journey* (1946) was a drama with Maureen O'Hara. Payne played a con man trying to swindle a widow in *Larceny* (1948). Two musicals harkened back to his singing heyday, oldies *Hello, Frisco, Hello* (1943) with Alice Faye and *The Dolly Sisters* (1945) with Betty Grable.

Mitchum, having adopted a tough guy persona, career boosted by his only Oscar nomination for Best Supporting Actor in *The Story of G.I. Joe* (1946), and now having eased his way into the moviegoer's affections, the actor shifted gears for *Holiday Affair* (1949), a romantic comedy with another rising star Janet Leigh. But in most of his other films showing in Paisley in 1950 he played to type. He appeared in a pair of film noir pictures, *The Big Steal* (1949), directed by Don Siegel (*Dirty Harry*), opposite Jane Greer and in Edward Dmytryk's *Crossfire* 1947). He packed his pistols in a trio of westerns: Robert Wise's *Blood on the Moon* (1948) with Barbara Bel Geddes, *Rachel and the Stranger* (1948) with Loretta Young and William Holden, and B picture *West of the Pecos* (1944). The two dramas could not have been more different. *The Red Pony* (1949) starring Myrna Loy was an adaptation of John Steinbeck's much loved novel while Raoul Walsh's *Pursued* (1947) with Teresa Wright was a more intense affair.

Joint 21st were **Betty Grable** (8 films, 28 days) and **Yvonne De Carlo** (6 films, 28 days). Betty Grable had been the top female star of the 1940s. In 1946 and 1947 she was one of the top three highest-paid stars in Hollywood. She was a famous World War II pinup and her legs were insured for a million dollars. For virtually the entire decade she made nothing but musicals and with each new song-and-dance epic her popularity grew. From 1942 to 1950 she appeared on the annual list of the Top Ten Box Office Stars as judged by cinema owners and managers. Beginning in 1942 in eighth spot, she leapt to the top position the following year; in successive years (1947 and 1948) she placed second; and three times (1944, 1945 and 1950) she was fourth. She was by far the most consistent female performer on the list. However, she did venture out of her chosen speciality in 1949 for the western *The Beautiful Blonde from Bashful Bend*. That film was shown in Paisley in 1950 but all the other films from her repertoire that year were musicals: *Wabash Avenue* (1950) with Victor Mature, *When My Baby Smiles at Me* (1948) with Dan Dailey, *The Dolly Sisters* (1945), *Song of the Islands* (1942) also with Mature, *Springtime in the Rockies* (1942) with Carmen Miranda, and *Moon over Miami* (1941) and *Down Argentine Way* (1940), both co-starring Don Ameche

Below: change of gear for tough guy Robert Mitchum in *Holiday Affair* (1949).

Canadian Yvonne De Carlo (real name Margaret Yvonne Middleton) was one Hollywood's fastest rising stars. Paisley audiences in 1950 could see her in swashbuckler *Buccaneer's Girl* (1950), comedy western *The Gal Who Took the West* (1949), offbeat western *Calamity Jane and Sam Bass* (1949), and film noir *Criss Cross* (1949) in which she played the ex-wife of Burt Lancaster who tries to save her from the Los Angeles underworld. She was teamed also up twice with Dan Duryea, as Lola Montes in *Black Bart: Highwayman* (1948) and action drama *River Lady* (1948) set in lumber territory.

William Holden (six films, 28 days) pinned down 23rd place. Although he had been around the Hollywood block for more than a decade he had failed to cement a spot among the industry's elite and had fallen so foul of studio Columbia that he had been suspended several times. Although he was on the verge of bigger things, at this stage in his career it would be hard to define what he brought to a picture, his persona not as solidified as, for example, newcomer Robert Mitchum. In a bid to reboot his career he had moved into comedy with *Father Is A Bachelor* (1950) with Colleen Gray, *Dear Wife* (1949) with Joan Caulfield, and *Innocence Is Bliss* (aka *Miss Grant Takes Richmond*, 1949) opposite Lucille Ball. But vestiges of his tougher characters were to be seen during 1950 in Paisley in western *Streets of Laredo* (1949), as the psychopathic killer taking a family hostage in *The Dark Past* (1948) with Nina Foch and western *Rachel and the Stranger* (1948).

Below: swashbuckling stars were usually men but Yvonne De Carlo broke the mould in *Buccaneer's Girl* (1950).

Six stars vied for 24th spot - **James Stewart** (6 films, 27 days), **Alan Ladd** (five films, 27 days) and **Spencer Tracy** (3 films, 27 days), **William Bendix** (five films, 27 days), **Jon Hall** (6 films, 27 days) and **Edward G. Robinson** (7 films, 27 days).

East of the Rising Sun (aka *Malaya*, 1949) led the way for James Stewart, the adventure picture co-starring Spencer Tracy and new Italian star Valentina Cortese along with baseball biopic *The Stratton Story* (1949) with June Allyson. He was also seen in Hitchcock's *Rope* (1948) and romance *You Gotta Stay Happy* (1948) with Joan Fontaine as well as *Magic Town* (1947) with Jane Wyman and a revival of western *Destry Rides Again* (1939) with Marlene Dietrich.

Alan Ladd as *The Great Gatsby* (1949) rivaled Errol Flynn in *The Forsyte Saga* as the most ambitious casting of the year. For those Paisley movie fans who preferred the actor in the more typical tough guy roles in which he had specialised since his breakthrough in film noir *This Gun for Hire* (1942), he also had on show *After Midnight* (aka *Captain Carey USA*, 1950) with Wanda Hendrix and *Appointment with Danger* (1950) with British star Phyllis Calvert. He also appeared in two films co-starring Donna Reed – the drama *Beyond Glory* (1949) and thriller *Chicago Deadline* (1948).

Of all the stars to make the Paisley Top 30 Spencer Tracy required the fewest films. His outstanding attracting was comedy *Adam's Rib*, his sixth coupling with Katharine Hepburn and directed by George Cukor, which won maximum playing time in the town's cinemas. Also showing were *East of the Rising Sun* (aka *Malaya*, 1949) and a revival of historical adventure *Northwest Passage* (1940).

William Bendix was the most unlikely of stars. In an era where most Hollywood idols were handsome, he was blessed with a mashed-up face. Theoretically, he should have been relegated to playing tough guys, but, instead, he proved as adept at comedy and biopics, essaying the baseball legend in *The Babe Ruth Story* (1948) and churning out the laughs in *The Life of Riley* (1949) and *Two Knights from Brooklyn* (1949). Paisley film noir fans in 1950 could enjoy him in *Race Street* (1948), *Johnny Holiday* (1949) and *Cover Up* (1949).

Jon Hall owed his exotic looks to his mother, a Tahitian princess, and that coupled with his onscreen virility brought him stardom is a series of adventure pictures including two with Dorothy Lamour, John Ford's *The Hurricane* (1937) and *Aloma of the South Seas* (1941), but by the end of the 1940s that genre had fallen out of fashion and so, to a large extent, had the actor, but he was still a big enough marquee name to attract audiences in Paisley. He was seen in western *Deputy Marshall* (1949) with his wife Frances Langford, action film *The Mutineers*

(1949) with Adele Jergens, *Last of the Redskins* (1947) - a remake of *Last of the Mohicans*, one of his biggest hits, and known in the U.S. as *Last of the Redmen* – comedy *San Diego, I Love You* (1944), and revivals of two of his previous successes *White Savage* (1943) with Maria Montez and *Kit Carson* (1940).

Edward G Robinson (seven films, 27 days) did not disappoint his Paisley fans in 1950 who had come to rely on their favourite in tough guy roles. He starred in film noir *House of Strangers* (1949) with Susan Hayward and John Huston's *Key Largo* (1948) with Humphrey Bogart. In a departure from the normal kind of role, he took the lead in the adaptation of Arthur Miller's play *All My Sons* (1948). He was seen in two films with Loretta Young, *Date with Destiny* (aka *The Stranger*, 1946) and *The Honourable Mr Wong* (aka *Hatchet Man*, 1932). Out of the vaults also came Raoul Walsh drama *Manpower* (1941) with Marlene Dietrich and John Ford's *Passport to Fame* (aka *The Whole Town's Talking*, 1935) with Jean Arthur.

Rounding out the Top 30 was **James Mason** (6 films, 25 days), the only British star to make the chart. For many years the number one male actor on this side of the Atlantic, he had now made the crossing to America where he was paired with a succession of established or up-and-coming female talent in a mixture of dramas and film noir. The fruits of his Hollywood adventure were on full display in Paisley in 1950 and without the imprimatur of

105

the big U.S. studios it is doubtful if the actor would have held such sway in a town that was notably averse to English actors. In terms of budget, MGM's *Madame Bovary* (1949), starring Jennifer Jones and directed by Vincente Minnelli from the classic French novel, was top of the heap. But running it close was romantic drama *East Side, West Side* (1949) in which Mason played a rich businessman caught between Barbara Stanwyck and Ava Gardner. Two of his film noirs were directed Max Ophuls, *Reckless Moment* (1949) opposite Joan Bennett and *Caught* (1949) with Barbara Bel Geddes while a third, set in Mexico, *One Way Street* (1950) also starred Swedish newcomer Marta Toren. To cash in on this influx of films, one of his most famous oldies was resurrected, *The Wicked Lady* (1945) with Margaret Lockwood.

An idea of the frequency with which actors appeared on the screens was the fact that a total of 77 movie stars could be seen in four or more movies in Paisley in 1950.

The Top B Movie Stars

As previously mentioned, cinemas during this period were not able to exist on a diet of high-budget Hollywood pictures and had to rely, to fill out a programme, on B pictures and reissues. Most of the movies did not top the bill but, instead, fulfilled the function of being the supporting movie. And the favoured stars of B movies formed a category all of their own. Western star **Wild Bill**

Elliott, for example, was to be seen in a total of seven movies, only two of which were the main attraction, the other five being the support including three "Red Ryder" films – *Cheyenne Wildcat* (1944), *The Great Stagecoach Robbery* (1945) and *Phantom of the Plains* (1945). In fact, only one of his films shown in Paisley in 1950 was made later than 1945. **William Boyd** was seen in 11 Hopalong Cassidy films, all of them supports, **Johnny Mack Brown** in seven westerns in the "Rough Riders" series, again all supports. **Penny Singleton** appeared in three "Blondie" pictures, based on the comic strip character, and again all were supports. However, the kinds of the reissues were **Laurel and Hardy**. Eleven of the duo's movies were on show, but only one, *Bohemian Girl* (1936), made it to the top of the bill. The others taking a repeat bow in Paisley in 1950 were: *Jailbirds* (aka *Pardon Us*, 1931), *Pack Up Your Troubles* (1932), *Wooden Soldiers* (aka *Babes in Toyland*, 1934), *Our Relations* (1936), *Flying Deuces* (1939), *Saps at Sea* (1940), *A Chump at Oxford* (1940), *A-Haunting We Will Go* (1942), *Jitterbugs* (1943), and *Air Raid Wardens* (1943).

Note: in compiling the Top 30, I ignored those stars of B films whose movies primarily acted as supporting features. Interestingly enough, it would not have excluded **Roy Rogers** since four films out of the five released in Paisley in 1950 were main attractions, and in terms of the numbers of days these represented would have allowed him to nestle just outside the Top 30.

Penny Singleton starred as "Blondie" in the titular series.

Chapter Four: Title Changes

The titles of Hollywood films were changed on a regular basis. The most common reason was to dupe the public into thinking they were seeing a new film, a practice so rampant in Hollywood that it provoked legal consequence and public outcry. So for this reason William Wyler's *Dead End* (1937) became *Crime's End* on reissue 13 years later. Frank Capra's *Meet John Doe* (1941) was reinvented as *John Doe Dynamite* and John Ford's *The Whole Town's Talking* (1935) starring Edward G. Robinson and Jean Arthur as *Passport to Fame*. Lon Chaney as *The Wolf Man* (1941) transformed into *Destiny*, and Bela Lugosi as *The Ape Man* (1943) into *The Gorilla Man*.

Other times it was to exploit the back catalogue of an actor/actress who had a big hit or had achieved newfound stardom such as Lana Turner whose *Two Girls on Broadway* (1940) transformed into *Choose Your Partner*. Dana Andrews in *Armored Attack* (1943) was now a bigger name so the film was relaunched as *North Star*. With Ingrid Bergman back on top in *Under Capricorn* (1949) and *Stromboli* (1950) her Hollywood debut *Intermezzo* (1939) was renamed *Escape to Happiness*. Laurel and Hardy comedies were so common on the reissue circuit that the only way to provide novelty was by name-change, hence *Pardon Us* (1931) reappeared as *Jailbirds* and *Babes in Toyland* (1934) as *Wooden Soldiers*. And the film did not have to be so old. *Colorado*

Territory (1948) starring Virginia Mayo returned a few months after initial release in 1950 as *North of the Rio Grande*.

Sometimes titles were changed for no reason that appeared obvious. *Adventures of Don Juan* in America became *The New Adventures of Don Juan*. Sometimes the reason was obvious. *The Forsyte Saga* was known as *That Forsyte Woman* in America in echo of Vivien Leigh-starrer *That Hamilton Woman*, but it retained the title of the book on which it was based when released in the U.K. Nobody in Britain could remember who *The Powers Girl* (1943) was and the biopic was re-titled *Hello, Beautiful*. Nor was there the slightest interest in baseball, so *Take Me to the Ball Game* (1949) starring Frank Sinatra and Esther Williams was launched as *Everybody's Cheering*. A "freshman" was not a term used in Britain so *Mother Was a Freshman* became *Mother Knows Best*. Nor could you imagine many people would understand the meaning behind *Johnny Allegro* (1949) starring George Raft so that switched to *Hounded*.

Changes were not always for the better. *Mr Soft Touch* sounded a pretty decent description of the Glenn Ford film noir whereas *House of Settlement* had no ring to it at all. With Lucille Ball and William Holden as the stars, *Miss Grant Takes Richmond* (1949) possibly seemed too aggressive for a simple romantic comedy so it turned into the more innocuous *Innocence Is Bliss*. There must have been a good reason to swap the title of *Dark City* (1950),

110

especially as it heralded as a career breakthrough for Charlton Heston, into *No Escape*

Titles that included obscure place names were often replaced, Randolph Scott western *Albuquerque* turning into *Silver City*, Louis Hayward swashbuckler *The Pirates of Capri* into *The Masked Pirate*.

But who knows what was so off-putting about *Malaya* (1949) with Spencer Tracy and James Stewart, possibly too close to another film incorporating the country into a title, and in any case *East of the Rising Sun* sounded a bit more dangerous. *The Fuller Brush Man* was not a concept known to the British audience so the Red Skelton comedy was whisked up into *That Mad Mr Jones*.

Chapter Five: Cinema History and Memory Studies

This book is not intended, per se, as an academic study, but it does have its place in the academic literature relating to Cinema History and Memory Studies.

The Paisley cinemagoing experience is unique to Paisley. The town had a preference for particular types of movies and, as importantly, as I have explained, for particular stars. Where else in the country, I should like to know, was there such a fondness for Virginia Mayo?

In terms of Cinema History (the study of what happened to movies after they were made rather than analysis of the content of the film), there is virtually no research on comparing city-by-city or town-by-town preferences or even to work out exactly how the cinema food chain actually worked in 1950 terms of which cities and towns received the preferential treatment.

This also brings into focus Film Memory Studies, which are gaining in popularity in the academic world. Although such studies generally involve as participants people who lived through the various eras in question, the researchers did not and so most of this kind of research is polarised, and viewed through the eyes of a researcher. Taking 1950 as an example, a researcher would be more familiar with pictures that were critically-acclaimed or widely popular such as *Winchester '73* or *On the Town*, and have a nodding acquaintance with, at the most, 50 or so movies, rather than a deeper understanding of the 1,200 movies that made up the cinemagoing diet of the people the researcher is trying to interview.

The surge of interest in film history memory-based studies would be assisted by the greater availability of context if the subject area is not to be submerged by allegations of "false" memory. Unlike other research programmes, memory-based studies are dependent on the particular. The person remembering going to the cinema must base such recollection on a particular town or city and a particular time. The time in question may be a very short window indeed, one year or a few years. However, the researcher in charge of asking the questions and thus prompting the answers has to take great care in ensuring that both questions and answers revolve around the same, and necessarily precise, context.

Taking the year 1950, for example, a researcher may rely on cinema history principles rather than context. In other words, a researcher might remember that 1950 spawned such Hollywood greats as *Broken Arrow* or *A Place in the Sun* etc without stopping to think whether such films were actually shown in the restricted locale available to the study clientele. This could result in "false" memory. The client might well easily recall the cinema that he or she visited, and other elements of the moviegoing experience, but that might be in general terms. However, it is equally possibly that the film – perhaps prompted by the researcher's questioning - they recalled seeing was one that they saw later, even perhaps on television. This is because, as this study shows, films were only available for

113

exceptionally short periods of time, by modern standards, in cinemas in smaller towns and even bigger cities outside of a capital city where a movie received its premiere showings in a major "first run" theatre. For example, *Broken Arrow*, the much-vaunted Delmer Daves western, considered one to have changed the shape of the genre, was only available to be seen in Paisley for three days each in two cinemas simultaneously (i.e. six days total) at the start of the week. So the possibility of the person being interviewed seeing that film would be much less likely than war picture *Battleground* or Danny Kaye in *Inspector General* which were both screened simultaneously in two cinemas for six days each (i.e. 12 days total including the busier weekend). In the context of a study, the interviewee might well "remember" seeing a film that it was more likely that, due to limited availability, they did not.

In terms of social study, it would help a researcher to know in which cinema the interviewee saw a particular film. Awareness of what was showing in a particular year in a given cinema would greatly assist this task. Some cinemas were more luxurious, and therefore expensive, and other cinemas were cheaper, and the decision to go to one or the other may depend on factors, such as courting, other than opting for which film to see. As it happened, I knew that a major new Europe-wide initiative in Film History covering the 1950s called "European Cinema Audiences" has just been launched and I was aware too of the growing interest in memory studies in relation to Blow: inemagoing and I realised that a book focused just

Below: one of the biggest hits of the year, yet *The Inspector General* (1949) is unlikely to come up in any Memory Study.

IN EVERY ONE OF ITS 270 DATES THE PHENOMENAL RECEIPTS NOW MAKE

DANNY KAYE

the Inspector General

IN COLOR BY Technicolor

THE ALL-TIME COMEDY KAYO FROM WARNER BROS.

on one small British town, albeit in almost obsessive detail, could provide the context and the technique of study that is often missing from this area, when researchers organising studies on what the audience saw really have little understanding of what they actually did see, or could have seen, beyond the prompting of an interviewer.

Note: the following programmes are arranged by month and by cinema. Two films making up a complete programme are separated by a forward slash (/) while an asterisk (*) is used to denote a new complete programme.

JANUARY 1950

ASTORIA
The Lone Wolf and a Lady / Rusty Saves a Life * The Dark Past / Black Eagle * The Noose Hangs High / Raw Deal * The Crime Doctor's Diary / Blondie's Secret * Sealed Verdict / She's No Lady * The Adventures of Casanova / Sealed Verdict * Beyond Glory / Some Like it Hot * You Gotta Stay Happy / New Frontier * Paper Orchid / Fatal Night

KELBURNE
The Dolly Sisters * Jungle Jim / Big Deal * Top o' the Morning / King of Chinatown * Red Canyon / The Melody Club * Without Reservations (Sunday only) * Maytime in Mayfair * The Three Musketeers * The Dangerous Age / The Rose of Youth

LA SCALA
Two Girls and a Sailor * Brewster's Millions / Flying Deuces * If You Knew Susie / West of Pecos * A Song Is Born * Chicago Deadline / Television Spy * The Secret Garden / Between Two Women * The Kissing Bandit * The Younger Brothers / Princess O'Rourke

NEW ALEX
Burning Cross / Dangerous Blondes * I Shot Jesse James / The Clancy St Boys * Man on the Run / Winner Takes All * Kid Dynamite / Buffalo Bill Rides Again * The Babe Ruth Story / Shanghai Chest * Marry Me / The Bowery at Midnight * Private Angelo / Fighting Fools * Spellbound / Thundering Trails * The Gay Desperado/A Man's Affairs

PALLADIUM
Racing Luck / Dangerous Blondes * The Gallant Blade / Fighting Joe Palooka * The Last Round Up * Murder at the Windmill / The Lady Is Willing * Sorrowful Jones * Law of the Barbary Coast / Out of the Storm * The Great Gatsby * The Contact Man * The Lone Wolf and a Lady / Sons of Adventure * The Streets of Laredo * Walk a Crooked Mile / Lady at Midnight * Springtime in the Sierras / Loser Takes All * The Captain from Castile

118

F. Scott Fitzgerald's classic novel *The Great Gatsby* (1949) starred tough guy Alan Ladd. A silent version had appeared in 1926.

PICTURE HOUSE
Chinese Adventure / The Schemer * Jungle Jim / Big Deal * The Last of the Redskins / Mary Lou * Paper Orchid / Hokus Pokus * Black Dragons / Spooks Run Wild * Manhandled / The King of Alcatraz * The Devil's Hand / The Brute Man

REGAL
My Dream Is Yours / The House Across the Street * Landfall/Bad Boy * Maytime in Mayfair * The Three Musketeers * Saints and Sinners / Argyle's Secret

WEST END
The Notorious Lone Wolf / Law of the Pampas * The Thrill of Brazil / The Clancy St Boys * Last of the Redskins / Mary Lou * Bad Men of Tombstone / Parole Inc * The Babe Ruth Story /Shanghai Chest * Marry Me / The Bowery at Midnight * The Feathered Serpent / The Strange Mrs Crane * Spellbound / Thundering Trails * The Brute Man / The Devil's Hand

FEBRUARY 1950

ASTORIA
Blood on My Hands / Drums Along the Amazon * The Secret Life of Walter Mitty * Silver City / Big Town after Dark * River Lady / Chumps at Oxford * Floodtide / Canon City * Ride 'Em Cowboy / The Monkey's Paw * Every Girl Should Be Married / Sunset Pass

KELBURNE
Rope of Sand * The Hasty Heart * Good Sam / Strange Bargain * Black Bart / Invisible Ghosts * Mother Knows Best / Roses Are Red * Rogues' Regiment / Moonlight in Hawaii

LA SCALA
Rope of Sand * Everybody's Cheering * Slattery's Hurricane / I Cheated the Law * Johnny Stoolpigeon / Trottie True * Take One False Step / Dear Mr Promack * When My Baby Smiles at Me * Madness of the Heart / Arctic Manhunt

120

Yvonne De Carlo played Lola Montez in western *Black Bart* (1948).

A huge hit for future U.S. president Ronald Reagan, *The Hasty Heart* (1949) also starred Patricia Neal and British actor Richard Todd who was nominated for a Best Actor Oscar.

NEW ALEX
One Rainy Afternoon / Celia * Find the Blackmailer / The Last Wild Horses * Golden Eye / Valley of Fear * Not Wanted / Loveable Cheat * Miraculous Journey / Queen of the Amazons * The Sirens of Atlantis / Urubu / The Dark Secret * Jigsaw / The Dead Don't Dream

PALLADIUM
Angel in Exile / Million Dollar Weekend * Black Eagle / Daredevils of the Clouds * That Mad Mr. Jones / Code of the Saddle * Force of Evil / Lost in a Harem * Last of the Redskins / Smuggler's Cove * The Secret Lady / My Hero * No Minor Vices / Air Raid Wardens * The Crime Doctor's Diary / Fighting Fools * Act of Violence / Choose Your Partner * Caught * Words and Music

PICTURE HOUSE
The Trouble Makers / Overland Trails * William Comes to Town / Here Comes Trouble * Ghosts in the Night / Fangs of the Wild * Good Sam / Strange Bargain * The Enchanted Valley / Joe Palooka in The Big Fight * Impact * Race Street / Magic Town

REGAL
Colorado Territory / Wallflower * The Hasty Heart * This Is the Army * The Man from 'Frisco / The Blue Scar * Any Number Can Play / Holiday in Havana * Incendiary Blonde / Niagara Falls

WEST END
The Trouble Makers / Overland Trails * Find the Blackmailer / The Last Wild Horses * Golden Eye / Valley of Fear * Not Wanted / Loveable Cheat * Miraculous Journey / Queen of the Amazons * The Enchanted Valley / Joe Palooka in The Big Fight * Dark Secret / The Ghost and the Guest * Magic Town / Race Street

123

MARCH 1950

ASTORIA
Some for the Boys / Rose of the Yukon * Eureka Stockade / Strange Confession * Moon over Miami / The Law of Timber * Rachel and the Stranger / Amazing Adventure * The Naughty Nineties / Men of San Quentin * Mr Blandings Builds a Dream House * Stagecoach / Dead Men Tell * Larceny / Vote for Huggett * You Only Live Once / The Cave Dwellers

KELBURNE
Lady Windermere's Fan / Kaura * The New Adventures of Don Juan * The Third Man * House of Strangers / Winners' Circle * Obsession * The Berkeleys of Broadway

LA SCALA
Meet the Ghosts / City across the River * On the Avenue / Mr Belvedere Goes to College * Dark Command * Tokyo Joe / Prison Warden * House of Strangers / Winners' Circle * Obsession * Lost People / Married But Single * The Velvet Touch / The Big Steal

NEW ALEX
Kidnapped / Law Comes to Gunsight * Voice of the Turtle * Rope / Granny Get Your Gun * For Them That Trespass / Henry the Rainmaker * Lucky Stiff / Sinister Journey * The Treasure of the Sierra Madre * Michael Halloran / The Music Man * Rebecca * Johnny Belinda

PALLADIUM
The Bribe * Shanghai Chest / The New Frontier * The Sun Comes Up * Three Godfathers * Fighting Back / Robin Hood of Monterey * Small Voice / The Feathered Serpent * When My Baby Smiles at Me * Tuna Clipper / King of the Gamblers * When William Comes Home / Borrowed Trouble * Saints and Sinners / Joe Palooka in the Big Fight * Night Wind / Valley of Fear * The Noose Hangs High / Parole Inc * Night Beat / Trouble Makers * Sword of the Avenger

124

PICTURE HOUSE
Diamond Frontier / Tough as They Come * Mother Riley's New Venture / Federal Fugitives * Kazan / The Make Believe Ballroom * Sun Town / San Francisco Docks * Bless Them All / Driftin' River * Champion / Fabulous Joe * Diamond Jim / No Way Back * A Date with Destiny / The Mutineers

REGAL
Interrupted Journey / Sofia * The New Adventures of Don Juan * The Third Man * In the Good Old Summertime * The Berkeleys of Broadway

WEST END
The Berkeleys of Broadway * Mother Riley's New Venture / Federal Fugitives * Poet's Pub /. Reign of Terror * Champion / Fabulous Joe * Michael Halloran / The Music Man * The Decision of Christopher Blake / The Hard Man * A Date with Destiny / The Mutineers

Below: Rosalind Russell in *The Velvet Touch* (1948).

APRIL 1950

ASTORIA
Tarzan and the Mermaids / Code of the West * Song of the Islands / Sundown * Tampico / The Jones Family in Hollywood * Kamsan / Secret Agent of Japan * Springtime in the Rockies / Deadline for Murder * Foreign Correspondent / Who Done It? * Passport to Pimlico / Love in Waiting * Kentucky / Johnny Comes Flying Home

KELBURNE
You Can't Sleep Here * Family Honeymoon / Don't Ever Leave Me * The Chiltern Hundreds / They Meet Again * Command Decision * The Great Lover / Big Brown Eyes * So Dear to My Heart / Showbusiness * Train of Events / Dinner at The Ritz * Tell it to the Judge / Hounded

LA SCALA
You Can't Sleep Here * The Red Pony / I Was a Convict * Run for Your Money / Big Cat * Command Decision * The Great Lover / Big Brown Eyes * So Dear to My Heart / Showbusiness * Mighty Joe Young

NEW ALEX
The Shop on Sly Corner / Strange Gamble * April Showers / The Hidden Hand * Flying Tigers / Valley of the Hunted Men * Storm over Bengal / Wagon Wheels West * My Girl Tisa / The Horn Blows at Midnight * Now Barabbas Was a Robber * Before I Hang / Crime's End

PALLADIUM
Mother Knows Best / The Challenge * Cover Up * Two Knights of Brooklyn / 13 Lead Soldiers * Champion / Fabulous Joe * The Conspirator * Captain Fury / Little Lost Men * You Can't Sleep Here * Impact / Susie Steps Out * Manhandled / The Mutineers * Too Late for Tears * The Secret Garden * Topper Takes a Trip / Chinese Adventure

PICTURE HOUSE
The File on Thelma Jordan / The Hunted Men * The Walking Hills / Two Blondes and a Redhead* Too Late for Tears / The Valiant

126

Hombre * The Lost Tribe / The Secret of St Ives * Miss Pilgrim / The North Star * Two Texas Knights / Shadows on the Stairs * Give Us This Day / Melody in the Dark * Tell it to the Judge / Hounded

REGAL
The Cure for Love * Crime School / The Honourable Mr. Wong * East of the Rising Sun / Hold That Baby * Look for the Silver Lining / Flaming Fury * Task Force / Alias the Champ

WEST END
The Shop on Sly Corner / Strange Gamble * April Showers / The Hidden Hand * The Chiltern Hundreds / Borrowed Trouble * The Lost Tribe / The Secret of St Ives * Miss Pilgrim / The North Star * My Girl Tisa / The Horn Blows at Midnight * Train of Events / Dinner at The Ritz * Before I Hang / Crime's End

Barbara Stanwyck goes film noir in *The File on Thelma Jordan* (1950).

MAY 1950

ASTORIA
Nobody Lives Forever / Charlie Chan in Reno * Thanks for Everything
/ My Son Alone * Whisky Galore / Fly Away Peter * The Verdict /
Charlie Chan in Monte Carlo * San Antonio * Jungle Jim * The Walking
Hills / The Oregon Trail * Perilous Holiday / Split Face * The Blue
Lagoon / King of the Turf

KELBURNE
Little Women * Jolson Sings Again * Under Capricorn * The Stratton
Story / The Golden Fleecing * Hello, Frisco, Hello / Scandal Sheet *
That Midnight Kiss

LA SCALA
Abbott and Costello Meet Boris Karloff / The Gal Who Took the West *
The Spider and the Fly / The Life of Riley * Scene of the Crime / When
Men Marry * Madame Bovary * Pinky * Everyone Does It/ Thieves
Highway * The Great Sinner * That Midnight Kiss

NEW ALEX
One Third of a Nation / The Treasure of Monte Carlo * Landfall /
Valiant Hombre * Bomba, Jungle Boy / Flashing Guns * The New
Adventures of Don Juan * Flamingo Road * To the Victor * Four Men
and a Prayer / City of Chance * Saddle Pals / The Streets of San
Francisco * The Younger Brothers/ Princess O'Rourke

PALLADIUM
Slattery's Hurricane / I Cheated the Law * Everybody's Cheering *
Song of the Indies / Chumps at Oxford * The Three Musketeers *
House of Strangers / Winners' Circle * The Dark Past / Bullets for
O'Hara * Mother Riley's New Venture / Federal Fugitives * The Snake
Pit * The Deep Valley * The Berkeleys of Broadway * Pitfall / Silent
Conflict * The Beast with Five Fingers / The Cheat * Command
Decision

128

PICTURE HOUSE
Under California Stars / Hideout * The Plunderers / The Duke of
Chicago * Jolson Sings Again * We Were Strangers / The Cheat *
Destry Rides Again / The Eyes of the Underworld * Hangman's Wharf
/ The Danny Kaye Story * Fighter Squadron / Gorilla Man * Escape
Me Never / Passage to Hong Kong

REGAL
Little Women * The Masked Pirate / Strangers Came * Angel with a
Trumpet / Flame of the Barbary Coast * Under Capricorn / The
Adventures of P.C. 49 * Fighting O'Flynn / Into the Straight * Twenty
Questions of Mystery / Bowery Bombshell * The Forsyte Saga

WEST END
Under California Stars / Hideout * The Plunderers / The Duke of
Chicago * Bomba, Jungle Boy / Flashing Guns * Homicide / The
Treasure of Monte Cristo * We Were Strangers / The Cheat * To the
Victor * Invisible Ghosts / The Danny Kaye Story * Saddle Pals / The
Streets of San Francisco * Winter Meeting

JUNE 1950

ASTORIA
The Lost Tribe / I Was a Convict * Shockproof / Wooden Soldiers *
Renegades / Arctic Manhunt * The Thief of Baghdad / Dick Tracy
Strikes Back * A Date with Destiny / Spooks Run Wild * The Big Sleep
* Undercover Man / Lunatics on Broadway * Drum / The Story of
Shirley Yorke * Reign of Terror

KELBURNE
Joan of Arc * East of Java / Calamity Jane and Sam Bass *
Undercover Man / Hitting the Jackpot* The Forsyte Saga * The
Rugged Riordans / The Buccaneer's Girl * Reckless Moment /
Innocence Is Bliss * Diamond City / Abandoned * Neptune's Daughter

Previous page: horror film *The Beast with Five Fingers* (1947)
starred Robert Alda, father of television star Alan Alda (*MASH*).

130

LA SCALA
Joan of Arc * Paid in Full / Dear Wife * Undercover Man / Hitting the Jackpot* After Midnight / McFadden's Flats * Reckless Moment / Innocence Is Bliss * Francis / A Woman in Hiding * The Blue Lamp

NEW ALEX
My Dream Is Yours * Down Argentine Way / Winner Takes All * An Old-Fashioned Girl / Jiggs and Maggie in Court * Twenty Questions Murder Mystery / Adam Had Four Sons * The Masked Pirate / Strangers Came * Sentimental Journey / Chasing Danger * Colorado Territory * It's Magic* Jesse James / Pardon Our Nerve

PALLADIUM
Silent Duet / The Strange Mrs Crane * Cheyenne * Red River * Rope of Sand * We Were Strangers * Chicago Deadline * Top o' the Morning * The Secret of St Ives / The Hidden Hand * Red, Hot and Blue / The Hunted Man * The File on Thelma Jordan * Silver River * The Great Lover / Special Agent * The Stratton Story

PICTURE HOUSE
Movie Crazy / Song of the Range * What a Carry On / A Touch of Shamrock * Voodoo Man / Block Busters * The Great Manhunt / Blondie's Hero * Forgotten Women / Leave it to Henry * Captain China / The Movie Go Round * The Temptress / The Marines Come Through * A Stranger Walked In / The Rats of Tobruk

REGAL
No Place for Jennifer / North West Stampede * White Heat * Your Witness / The Man in Black * Neptune's Daughter

WEST END
Movie Crazy / Song of the Range * What a Carry On / A Touch of Shamrock * An Old-Fashioned Girl / Jiggs and Maggie in Court * Voodoo Man / Block Busters * The Great Manhunt / Blondie's Hero * Forgotten Women / Leave it to Henry * A Kiss for Corliss / The Yank Comes Back * St Martin's Lane / The Man from Texas * A Stranger Walked In / The Rats of Tobruk

131

Lizabeth Scott (born Emma Matzo) appeared in two films in 1950, the drama *Paid in Full* (above) and *Dark City* opposite Charlton Hesaton.

ASTORIA
My Reputation / Wagon Wheels Westward * Tulsa / Flaming Fury *
Lust for Gold / Mary Lou * Criss Cross / Saddle Pals * The Wake of the
Red Witch / Queen of the Seas * Mexican Hayride / Storm over Bengal
* Knock on Any Door / Air Hostess * The Lady Gambles / North West
Trail

KELBURNE
Three Came Home / It Happens Every Spring * Come to the Stable *
White Heat * You're My Everything * Tarzan's Magic Fountain / Make
Mine Laughs * A Holiday Affair / Dangerous Profession * For Love of
Mary / The Adventures of Jane * San Diego, I Love You / Private
Buckeroo

LA SCALA
Return of the Bad Men / Back Bait * Gunga Din * Ma and Pa Kettle /
Madonna of the Seven Moons * Irish Eyes Are Smiling * You're My
Everything * Tarzan's Magic Fountain / Make Mine Laughs * A Holiday
Affair / Dangerous Profession * Swanee River / Desert Victory *
Stromboli / The Girl from Texas

NEW ALEX
A Matter of Murder / The Devil's Playground * Home Stretch / Sing and
Be Happy * Key Largo * Whiplash / Shadows on the Stair * Ride,
Ryder, Ride / Shamrock Hill * Project X / Captain Caution * Invisible
Ghosts / The Man from Texas * John Loves Mary / Smart Girls Don't
Talk * June Bride

PALLADIUM
Captain China / The King of Alcatraz * Little Women * The Walking
Hills * In the Good Old Summertime * Any Number Can Play * The Big
Punch * The Great Sinner * Everybody Does It / The Dangerous Years
* Adventure Island / Our Relations * East of the Rising Sun * Hello,

133

Frisco, Hello * Rose of the Yukon / Golden Eye * Whisky Galore / Feudin', Fussin', Fightin'

PICTURE HOUSE
Man Without a Conscience / The Black Raven * Undertow / Yes, Sir, That's My Baby * Home of the Brave / The Gay Amigo * School for Randle / Hay Foot * Down Dakota Way / The Flame of Youth * There's a Girl in My Heart / Angels in Disguise * Mary Ryan, Detective / Dangerous Inheritance * House of Settlement / Beware of Blondie

REGAL
Chain Lightning / Strike it Rich * It's a Great Feeling / Deputy Marshall * The Fighting Kentuckian / Arson Inc. * The Countess of Monte Cristo / Love Story * Adam's Rib / Shep Come Home * South of St Louis / Kissing in the Dark

WEST END
A Matter of Murder / The Devil's Playground * Undertow / Yes, Sir, That's My Baby * Come to the Stable / Rope of Sand * Assassin / Search for Danger * Undertow / Yes, Sir, That's My Baby * Down Dakota Way / The Flame of Youth * There's a Girl in My Heart / Angels in Disguise * Trade Wings

AUGUST 1950

ASTORIA
Flying Tigers / The Valley of Hunted Men * The Red Pony / The Gangs of Chicago * City across the River / Alias the Champ * Abandoned / Diamond City * Rogue Regiment / Moonlight in Hawaii* The Big Cat / Run for Your Money * The Gal Who Took the West * The Streets of San Francisco

KELBURNE
Copper Canyon / Lady Be Careful * All the Kings' Men * Madeleine * It's a Great Feeling / South of Suez * Under My Skin / Canadian Pacific * The Golden Salamander / Free for All * My Foolish Heart

LA SCALA

134

Copper Canyon / Lady Be Careful * Twelve O'Clock High * Riding
High * Appointment with Danger * My Foolish Heart * Back to Bataan

NEW ALEX
Two Texan Knights / Gorilla Man * The Decision of Christopher Blake /
Flaxy Martin * The Boys in Brown / The Story of Molly X * The Rocking
Horse Winner / Trapped * The Hasty Heart / Movie Crazy / Song of the
Range * Massacre River / Alimony * Hellfire / Escape to Happiness *
Daughter of the Jungle / Lone Texas Ranger

PALLADIUM
Pinky * Storm over Bengal / Overland Trails * That Midnight Kiss *
Canon City * Hideout / Michael O'Halloran * Scene of the Crime /
Within the Law * Madame Bovary * Knock on Any Door * The Prince of
Foxes * Come to the Stable / Rope of Sand * Night Train to Nevada /
Dragon * Thieves Highway / Jitterbugs * Third Time Lucky / The
Wistful Widow of Wagon Gap

PICTURE HOUSE
Tension / Women Against Women * All the Kings Men / Three Ham on
Rye * The Wicked Lady / Nitwit on Parade * Indian Scout / The Great
Dan Patch * Up for the Cup / For You I Die * And Baby Makes Three /
Old Smoky * Outpost in Morocco / Africa Screams

REGAL
Young Man of Music / The Blonde Bandit * Ambush / Side Street *
Guilt Is My Shadow / Mickey * Lost Boundaries / The Body Said No *
Double Confession / Stampede * The Last Holiday / Room To Let

WEST END
The Boys in Brown / The Story of Molly X * The Rocking Horse Winner
/ Trapped * Indian Scout / The Great Dan Patch * Up for the Cup / For
You I Die * Massacre River / Alimony * Hellfire / Escape to Happiness
* Daughter of the Jungle / Lone Texas Ranger

Robert Young and Barbara Hale in *And Baby Makes Three* (1949)

ASTORIA
The Life of Riley / The Spider and The Fly * Dark Command / The Treasure of Monte Cristo * Black Bart / San Francisco Docks * Diamond Frontier / Tough As They Come * Abbott and Costello Meet the Ghosts / The Last of the Wild Horses * White Savage / Wake Up and Dream * The Adventures of Martin Eden / I Shot Jesse James * Francis / Ringside

KELBURNE
South of St Louis / A Kiss in the Dark * The Doctor and The Girl / Free and Easy * No Man of Her Own * Dance Hall / Destiny * At the Circus / A-Haunting We Will Go * Mark of the Gorilla / No Escape * Battleground

LA SCALA
Morning Departure * No Man of Her Own * Baghdad / Borderline * The Beautiful Blonde from Bashful Bend / The Keys of the Kingdom * Dancing in the Dark / Father Was a Full Back * Cheaper by the Dozen

NEW ALEX
Man Proof / North West Passage * China Caravan * C Men / Shoot to Kill * The Last of the Mohicans / Harpoon * The Adventures of Gallant Bess / Mississippi Rhythm * The Bohemian Girl / Inner Sanctum * No Place for Jennifer / Northwest Stampede * The Panther's Claw / Inside the Law

PALLADIUM
Flying Tigers * Floodtide / Larceny * The Forsyte Saga * Tulsa / Homicide * Criss Cross / Whiplash * You're My Everything * Mexican Hayride / Mary Ryan, Detective * Twelve O'Clock High * The Golden Salamander / The Life of Riley * The Great Dan Patch / Gas Squad * Africa Screams / Outpost in Morocco * Cry Wolf / Illegal Entry * Indian Scout / Prison Warden

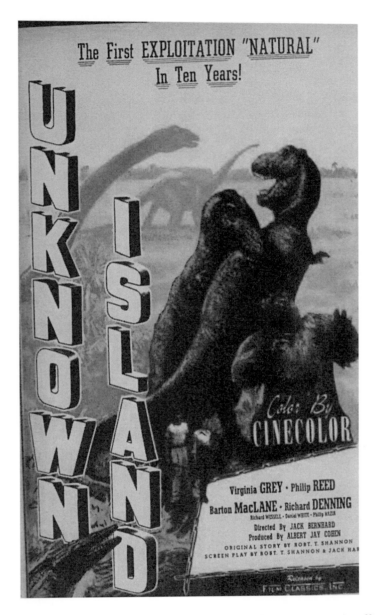

Monsters run amok in *Unknown Island* (1948), a *King Kong* rip-off.

PICTURE HOUSE

The Crooked Way / False Paradise * Zamba the Gorilla / King of the Bandits * The Big Wheel / The Daring Caballero * High Jinks in Society / Overland Riders * Torment / Wild City * Mark of the Gorilla / The Sea Wall * Wolf Hunter / Back Trail * Skimpy in the Navy / The Ghost of Hidden Valley

REGAL

The Happiest Days of My Life / Celia * The Search / Saps at Sea * Unknown Island / Slightly Honourable * The Eagle and The Hawk / The Dividing Line * Battleground

WEST END

The Romantic Age / Frisco Sal * Zamba the Gorilla / King of the Bandits * C Men / Shoot to Kill * The Last of the Mohicans / Harpoon * The Adventures of Gallant Bess / Mississippi Rhythm * The Bohemian Girl / Inner Sanctum * Wolf Hunter / Back Trail * The Panther's Claw / Inside the Law

OCTOBER 1950

ASTORIA

Give Us This Day / The Gunman's Code * Crossfire / Blonde Bandit * Riding High * Woman in Hiding / Song of the Sarong * The Red Canyon / The Melody Club * East of Java / San Diego, I Love You * Blood on the Moon / Follow Me Quietly * Abbott and Costello Meet the Killer, Boris Karloff / The Law of the Pampas * The Third Man / Ryder of the Plains

KELBURNE

Night and the City * Wabash Avenue * The Pride of Kentucky / The Girl from Jones Beach * Once More, My Darling / Prelude to Fame * So Long at the Fair / Outside the Wall * Nocturne (Sunday only) * The Big Lift * The Happiest Days of Your Life / The Great Stagecoach Robbery * The Dancing Years / 16 Fathoms Deep

139

LA SCALA
Night and the City * Wabash Avenue * Challenge to Lassie / Big Jack * Shadow on the Wall / Intruder in the Dust * Oh, You Beautiful Doll / Mother Didn't Tell Me * The Red Danube * They Were Not Divided * The Reluctant Widow / I Was a Shop Lifter

NEW ALEX
Escape Me Never / The Forgotten Woman * Winter Meeting / Leave it to Henry * Celia / Angels in Disguise * Fighter Squadron * Under Capricorn / Youth Takes a Hand * Your Witness * It's a Great Feeling / Passage from Hong Kong * Black Midnight / Under Arizona Skies * White Heat

PALLADIUM
Neptune's Daughter * Home of the Brave * Dark Command * The Big Wheel * Manpower / The Gunman's Code * Abbott and Costello Meet the Ghosts * The Beautiful Blonde from Bashful Bend / Bungalow 13 * The Crooked Way / False Paradise * The Big Cat / Bad Men of Missouri * Cheaper by the Dozen * Three Came Home / It Happens Every Spring * The Naked City / The Sea Wall / Now Barabbas Was a Robber

PICTURE HOUSE
Brimstone / The Animal Kingdom * John Doe, Dynamite (aka Meet John Doe) / Amazon * Loaded Pistols / Chinatown at Midnight * Anna Lucasta / Rusty's Birthday * In a Lonely Place / Father Is a Bachelor * The Big Lift * The Good Humor Man / Sentence Suspended * Over the Garden Wall / My Son The Hero

REGAL
Hollywood Canteen * The Girl Who Wouldn't Quit / Without Honour * The Pride of Kentucky / The Girl from Jones Beach * North West Mounted Police / Father to Son * Too Dangerous to Love / Embraceable You * East Side, West Side / Counter Punch * The Dancing Years / 16 Fathoms Deep

Right: Ida Lupino in film noir *Woman in Hiding* (1950).

WEST END
Brimstone / Strong Is the Seed * The Housekeeper's Daughter / Of
Mice and Men * The Underpup / An Elephant Never Forgets * Anna
Lucasta / Rusty's Birthday * In a Lonely Place / Father Is a Bachelor *
So Long at the Fair / Outside the Wall * The Fountainhead * Black
Midnight / Under Arizona Skies * Over the Garden Wall / My Son The
Hero

NOVEMBER 1950

ASTORIA
Calamity Jane and Sam Bass * Copper Canyon / McFadden's Flats *
The Pride of the Yankees / Studio Stoops * Buccaneer's Girl / The
Rugged O'Riordans * The Daltons Ride Again / The Winslow Boy *
Ruthless / School for Randle * The Plainsman / Niagara Falls * Ma and
Pa Kettle / Madonna of the Seven Moons * Here Come the Co-Eds /
Pursuit to Algiers *

KELBURNE
She Wore a Yellow Ribbon / Bride for Sale * One Way Street / Ma and
Pa Kettle Go to Town * On the Town * The Skipper Surprised His Wife
* Stars in My Crown / The Yellow Cab Man * The Lives of a Bengal
Lancer * The Adventures of Ichabod and Mr Toad / Capture

LA SCALA
Double Crossbones / Deported * She Wore a Yellow Ribbon * The
Black Hand / I'll Wait for You * One Touch of Venus / Men of Texas *
Louisa / Commanche Territory * Please Believe Me / Congo Maisie *
The Prisoner of Zenda * The Boy with the Green Hair / Top Hat * The
Adventures of Ichabod and Mr Toad / Capture

NEW ALEX
Stranger at My Door / Pack Up Your Troubles * Look for the Silver
Lining * Wallflower / One Last Fling * Chain Lightning * Task Force *
Roll, Thunder, Roll / Jackpot Jitters * The House by the River / The Kid
from Cleveland * The Fountainhead * South of St Louis

PALLADIUM
Adam's Rib * The Treasure of the Sierra Madre * Wabash Avenue *
After Midnight * Abbott and Costello Meet the Killer, Boris Karloff *
Challenge to Lassie / Big Jack * Night and the City * All My Sons / The
Devil's Henchman * Pursued * No Man of Her Own * T Men / No
Escape * The Red Danube * Shadows on the Wall / Intruder in the
Dust

PICTURE HOUSE
The Shark God / The Phantom Valley * Champagne for Caesar /
Satan's Cradle * The Golden Gloves Story / Father Makes Good *
Black Magic * D.O.A. * No Sad Songs for Me / A Woman of
Distinction * Ellen / Man of Courage * Mrs Mike / The Road to
Hollywood

REGAL
The Key to the City / Black Stallion * On the Town * Montana / Always
Leave 'Em Laughing * Cairo Road / Quiet Weekend

WEST END
Stranger at My Door / Pack Up Your Troubles * Champagne for
Caesar / Satan's Cradle * The Golden Gloves Story / Father Makes
Good * Black Magic * D.O.A. * Roll, Thunder, Roll / Jackpot Jitters *
The House by the River / The Kid from Cleveland * Ellen / Man of
Courage * Mrs Mike / The Road to Hollywood

Below: the second out of seven in the "Ma and Pa Kettle" series.

143

James Stewart starred in Delmer Daves' *Broken Arrow* **(1950).**

144

DECEMBER 1950

ASTORIA
Mighty Joe Young * The Navy Steps Out / Blonde Ice * Dangerous Profession / Holiday Affair * Private Buckeroo / They Live By Night * Stallion West / Melody Time * Sin Town / Tanks a Million* The Prisoner of Zenda / The Vagabond Love * Three Little Girls in Blue / The Argyle Secrets

KELBURNE
The Inspector General * Panic in the Streets * Broken Arrow * The Key to the City * Ticket to Tomahawk * Treasure Island * Tony Draws a Horse / Never Fear

LA SCALA
The Furies / My Friend Irma * Panic in the Streets * Broken Arrow * Leave Her to Heaven / The Lodger * The Black Rose * Treasure Island

NEW ALEX
The Girl from Jones Beach / The House across the Street * Trail of the Yukon / It's a Small World* He Stayed for Breakfast / Amazon * Let's Get Married / Jailbirds * Passport to Fame / Outlaws of the Orient * Young Man of Music * Always Leave Them Laughing / North of the Rio Grande * Unknown Island / Appointment with Murder

PALLADIUM
Tap Roots * Tension * The Search * He Walked by Night / Phantom of the Plains * Battleground / Dancing in the Dark / Father Was a Full Back * The Noose Hangs High / Alias the Champ * Oh, You Beautiful Doll / Mother Didn't Tell Me * When Willie Came Marching Home

PICTURE HOUSE
Chance of a Lifetime / Cheyenne Wildcat * Bowery Champs / Three of a Kind * The Last Bandit / Post Office Investigation * Johnny Holliday * Laughing Lads / Old Mother Riley's Circus * The Gay Ranchero / Unmasked * Night of Fame / The Clown * Kit Carson

REGAL
The Inspector General * The Gorbals Story / Take the Stage * One Sunday Afternoon / Barricade* The Wooden Horse / Monkey Manners

WEST END
Chance of a Lifetime / Cheyenne Wildcat * Trail of the Yukon / It's a Small World * The Last Bandit / Post Office Investigation * Johnny Holliday / Jailbirds * Highway 13 / Let Us Live * Gay Ranchero / Unmasked * Night of Fame / The Clown * Hello, Beautiful / The League of Frightened Men

Below: Dorothy McGuire in comedy *Mother Didn't Tell Me* (1950).

LIST OF ILLUSTRATIONS

Amira Moustafa was Zita, *Queen of the Amazons* (1947).

The Treasure of the Sierra Madre, advert, *Box Office*, December 27, 1947.

No Man of Her Own, advert, *Box Office*, April 29, 1950.

Black Magic, advert, *Box Office*, May 14, 1949.

Holiday Affair, advert, *Motion Picture Daily*, December 27, 1949.

Buccaneer's Girl, advert, *Motion Picture Daily*, March 16, 1950.

Blondie, advert, *Box Office*, November 19, 1938.

The Inspector General, advert, *Box Office*, January 14, 1950.

The Great Gatsby, advert, *Box Office*, January 8, 1949.

Black Bart, advert, *Box Office*, Jan 6, 1948.

The Hasty Heart, advert, *Box Office*, December 17, 1949.

The Velvet Touch, advert, *Box Office*, August 14, 1948.

The File on Thelma Jordan, advert, *Motion Picture Daily*, December 12, 1949.

The Beast with Five Fingers, advert, *Box Office*, January 4, 1947.

Paid in Full, advert, *Box Office*, April 8, 1950.

And Baby Makes Three, Pressbook.

Unknown Island, advert, *Motion Picture Daily*, December 14, 1948.

Woman in Hiding, advert, *Motion Picture Daily*, December 20, 1949.

Ma and Pa Kettle Go to Town, advert, *Box Office*, March 11, 1950.

Broken Arrow, advert, *Motion Picture Daily*, May 1, 1950.

Mother Didn't Tell Me, advert, *Box Office*, January 28, 1950.

Queen of the Amazons, advert, *Box Office*, February 1, 1947.

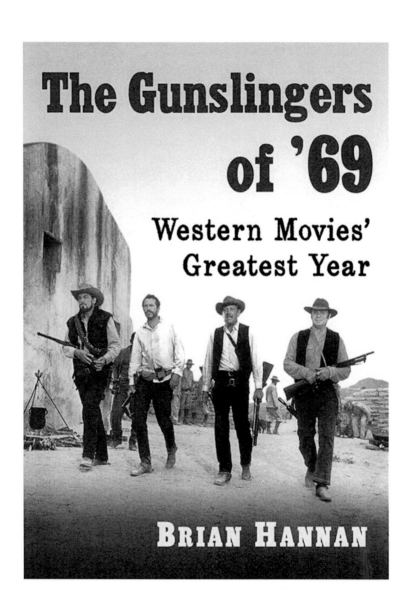

The Gunslingers of '69

Western Movies' Greatest Year

BRIAN HANNAN